THE MILLER │ HULL PARTNERSHIP   PUBLIC WORKS

The Miller|Hull Partnership
Public Works

PRINCETON ARCHITECTURAL PRESS, NEW YORK

Published by

Princeton Architectural Press

37 East 7th Street, New York, NY 10003

For a free catalog of books, call 1 (800) 722-6657

Visit our website at www.papress.com

Editor: Lauren Nelson Packard

Design Concept: Arnoud Verhaeghe and Paul Wagner

Layout: Miller | Hull

Special thanks to: Nettie Aljian, Bree Apperley, Sara Bader, Nicola Bednarek,
Janet Behning, Becca Casbon, Carina Cha, Penny (Yuen Pik) Chu, Carolyn Deuschle,
Russell Fernandez, Pete Fitzpatrick, Wendy Fuller, Jan Haux, Clare Jacobson,
Aileen Kwun, Nancy Eklund Later, Linda Lee, Laurie Manfra, John Myers,
Katharine Myers, Dan Simon, Andrew Stepanian, Jennifer Thompson, Joseph Weston,
and Deb Wood of Princeton Architectural Press
—Kevin C. Lippert, publisher

Library of Congress Cataloging-in-Publication Data

Miller/Hull Partnership

The Miller/Hull Partnership : public works / the Miller/Hull Partnership. — 1st ed.

   p.   cm.

ISBN 978-1-56898-754-5 (alk. paper)

1. Miller/Hull Partnership. 2. Architecture—United States—History—21st century.

3. Public buildings—United States. I. Title.

NA737.M49A4 2009

725.092'2—dc22

                                        2008047991

CONTENTS

Architects endure all the difficulties involved in raising buildings—artifacts that perhaps at first can be said to reflect our intentions, express our desires, and represent the problems we discuss in schools. For a time, we regard our buildings as mirrors; in their reflection we recognize who we are, and eventually who we were. We are tempted to think that a building is a personal statement within the ongoing process of history; but today I am certain that once the construction is finished, once the building assumes its own reality and its own role, all those concerns that occupied the architects and their efforts dissolve....The building itself stands alone, in complete solitude—no more polemical statements, no more troubles. It has acquired its definitive condition and will remain alone forever, master of itself....[W]hen architects realize that a building masters its own life, their approach to design is different....Our personal concerns become secondary and the final reality of the building becomes the authentic aim of our work. It is the building's materiality, its own being, that becomes the unique and exclusive concern.

Rafael Moneo, *The Solitude of Buildings*, 1986

FOREWORD

In the 1980s the influential thinker and educator Donald Schön used the environment of an architectural design studio to study educational methodology. He coined the term "reflective practice" to describe a practitioner (or group) who understands that his or her "expert" knowledge base is continuously changing from one circumstance to the next. The reflective practitioner therefore constantly reevaluates the process with the undertaking of each new enterprise. It must be understood that this is far removed from the ubiquitous corporate "mission statement," which reconciles profits with customer satisfaction. Though much debated over the years, the essence of Schön's idea is clear: in a society where a profession that serves the public (such as architecture) is subject to intense and sudden shifts in cultural ground, one must perpetually "reflect" on the status of the work and the means of its production. Thus the practitioner retains an awareness of such cultural shifts without being drawn into them. Schön referred to this as "reframing" a problem, suggesting it as the most successful means toward the realization of innovative attitudes and approaches.

Kenneth Frampton first applied this notion to architects, when he suggested that such an architectural practice might successfully resist the pull of two antithetical poles currently dominating the profession: "celebrity" firms that consider architecture a means of personal expression akin to the fine arts and "service" firms that accommodate basic building needs for profit. The Pacific Northwest firm of Miller|Hull is an archetypal example of a reflective practice, as evidenced not only by the body of work presented in this book—and the critical manner in which they chose to assemble it—but by the nature and structure of their office. Remarkably, in this age when narcissistic "starchitects" dominate the press, they achieve a poetic architecture that is both profound and comprehensible. By employing a vocabulary inclusive in character, they seamlessly close a gap frequently encountered in American public architecture: that between an inscrutable architectural syntax and the people it was created to serve. Thus a Miller|Hull building is comprehensible to its users yet uncompromisingly innovative in spirit and form. Because their values derive from fundamental design principles, advanced technologies in their work never dominate as stylistic effects. Instead, they are employed as part of a larger strategy to more deeply connect people to their place of work or home and—more importantly—to one another and the landscape/cityscape they inhabit.

As Miller|Hull shifts its attention to the design of larger public buildings, the firm's long-established skills at creating powerful and distinctive private spaces gives their public work qualities of scale and comfort so often lacking in projects of this size. For, in some way, every successful building that accommodates humans contains attributes of the concept of "house." Firms that produce public work without ever having mastered the making of houses all too often end up designing buildings that—though well-constructed and aesthetically orderly—lack scale, character, and a sense of well-being. Miller|Hull's private residences of the past twenty-five years are recognized worldwide as masterpieces of regional modernism infusing tradition with contemporary design and technology. This prelude to the firm's current focus on public buildings has clearly served them well.

The buildings and projects included in this book reveal Miller|Hull's skill and enthusiasm for making architecture in the public realm. Looking at them, one sees not only their strength of character and sense of belonging to the occupants, but also the excitement and promise of future public buildings and landscapes that will use them as lessons for reevaluation, enrichment, and growth. One is reminded of Picasso's famous response when asked which of his paintings was his favorite ("the next one"), for in the tactile materiality of these buildings can be found the outlines of spaces yet to be made. Though grounded in certain idealistic principles, the promise of these forthcoming spaces is boundless, for this is a firm whose very essence is to continuously evolve with the opportunities each new project presents.

J. M. Cava, architect
Portland, Oregon

INTRODUCTION

> Postmodern life could be described as a state in which everything beyond our own personal biography seems vague, blurred and somehow unreal. The world is full of signs and information which stands for things that no one fully understands because they, too, turn out to be mere signs for other things. Yet the real thing remains hidden. No one ever gets to see it. Nevertheless, I am convinced that real things do exist, however endangered they may be.
>
> Peter Zumthor, *Thinking Architecture,* 1997

In a setting where the virtual is increasingly shaping our lives and simulated environments provide backdrops that are becoming more influential by the day, the reality that is inherent in architecture can easily appear to remain hidden. In this context the significance of earth, water, natural light, gravity, and materials together with the importance of tools can provide anchors in what seems to be a rapidly swirling tide flooded by ideas and images, fashion and the apparently insatiable need for the new. The impact of this tide is perhaps most noticeable in the rapidly built landscapes that are being created in Asia and the Gulf. However it is also deeply embedded in the culture of modern architecture in the United States, where the market economy continues to exert an overwhelming force. Through the development of their work, The Miller|Hull Partnership is systematically engaged in a search for the real that establishes a welcome resistance.

Founders David Miller and Bob Hull studied architecture in the late sixties and early seventies against a backdrop defined by Frank Lloyd Wright, Buckminster Fuller, Ian McHarg, Louis Kahn, and an assortment of tools and techniques set out in the *Whole Earth Catalog.* Subsequently they went on to serve as Peace Corps Volunteers in Brazil and Afghanistan, respectively, and at a time when the United States was mesmerized by civil unrest at home and a war in Vietnam they established values based on thinking and doing. Firmly grounded in reality, those experiences were to provide a foundation for the practice that they established in 1977.

Like many emerging practices, theirs was dedicated to the design of modest houses and tiny cabins that provided weekend boltholes in remote forests or on islands overlooking expansive natural landscapes. These buildings were reminders of the primitive hut, which is at the origin of architecture. However the cabin in North America also recalls other important concerns in that initial moment of settlement—times when siting was not seen as a romantic engagement with nature but an action that was critical for survival, when materials were often scarce and consequently used frugally and ingeniously, when those materials were worked intensively by hand and frequently assembled by the same people who would occupy the finished building. And while today's cabin is more likely to be a recreational place that is used occasionally and fully equipped with the latest amenities, it continues to connect with those different histories and provide a basis for fundamental reconsiderations of space, construction, materials, natural systems, and ways of working.

In discussing ways of working, Renzo Piano has spoken of how he "cannot start a project from its theoretical framework and then work my way to the detail. I always follow a double process, I try to comprehend the ideological reasons for the project, what lies behind it, what constitutes its social and formal innovation, its functional requirements, the context within which one works with respect to fellow practitioners, and at the same time I find it difficult to divorce these issues from my initial design sketches on grubby bits of paper which I take everywhere, with designs of junctions, bolts, the smallest details. I cannot separate the two."[1] This idea of a double process resonates in the work of Miller|Hull. And while modest projects, like the Girvin Cabin on Decatur and the Marquand Retreat in Naches River Valley, continue to inspire work as the practice has grown, its approach to the design of larger buildings has continued to focus on that connection between a theoretical framework and grubby bits of paper, and refine the linkages that fuse concept and detail.

Using a limited palette of materials, the systems that it devises to make those buildings—structure, servicing, and enclosures—are all made clearly visible. In addition the details of those assemblies are elegant, painstakingly detailed, and thoughtfully integrated. These are characteristics that highlight the firm's resistance to many of the current practices that surround it. As a consequence the architecture of Miller|Hull contrasts sharply with much contemporary building in the United States where seemingly endless layers of drywall and suspended ceilings are used to conceal systems, reduce quality, and wrap space in generic ways that blur reality and create a nationwide sense of anomie. As the size and complexity of its commissions have increased, so Miller|Hull continues to aggressively explore integrative design. However that exchange has become more complex as it has involved working with a more diverse group of people and the recognition of the particular contributions that can be made by those different participants. In exchanging the private world of the house for the civic spaces of larger buildings, they have sought to reinterpret the programs so as to highlight the value and importance of public work.

Commenting on the education of an architect and the significance of programming space, Louis Kahn noted that "our profession is shabby only because we do not change the programming [of buildings]. If you change that programming, you release wonderful forces because the individual then never makes the mistake of making something which just pleases himself. You please society in your programming." He went onto to suggest that through "the rewriting of programming architecture can be detected."[2]

Over the years Miller|Hull has explored the "rewriting of programming." For example, the design of a public service building in a small town in Oregon was prompted by the need to improve water supply and treatment systems for a growing community. With a need for laboratories, storage of additional equipment, maintenance workshops, and staff workspace, this commission was viewed primarily as an upgrade of existing municipal facilities. However by carefully rewriting the program, it also became a place where architecture could be detected. Miller|Hull immediately began to work closely with the client, and, in its subsequent conversations with service engineers, infrastructure planners, and landscape architects, was able to develop a plan that would not only provide the additional space required but also refocus the project on the reality of water.

By envisioning the new building for the Wilsonville Water Treatment Plant as a wall, the designers were able to define a distinct front and back on the otherwise open site. This in turn enabled the client to make the building into a place where the very same water that was the raison d'etre for the project also became the focus of a new and extensive public landscape. Developing the design they were able to create that landscape alongside the building, which was part of the infrastructure of the water supply yet also intertwined with a network of public footpaths around a newly routed stream, which mirrored the flow of the water being treated inside the building. As a consequence this project became not only a facilities improvement but the catalyst for a significant new civic amenity. In a country where architecture is frequently directed towards the construction of privatized worlds, this project made a building that suddenly became a conspicuously public work.

Piano has suggested that "one of the disasters of our profession is that there is much talk of interdisciplinary activity but in effect it does not exist. There is a cascade relationship between different disciplines, so that one expert does something, then passes it on to someone else, and so on, but rarely does one experience a coming and going relationship."[3] Miller|Hull is increasingly basing the development of its way of working on "coming and going." Other commissions were conspicuously shaped by exchange, like the design of a new Environmental Services Building for Pierce County in the state of Washington located on a vast 700 acre site that was formerly a quarry. Here the "comings and goings" connect an increasingly diverse group of experts who project the professional boundaries far beyond those of the traditional building design team. The architects worked alongside geologists and historians, civil engineers and landscape architects, state and county legislators, political leaders, and community activists.

Gravel had been excavated from this extensive tract of land overlooking the Puget Sound by private companies for more than one hundred years, and consequently the site had been stripped of both soil and vegetation. Completely barren, it was acquired from the private owner by Pierce County in 1992 and a plan developed by a team headed by architects Arai Jackson. That master plan outlined the reclamation of the site, an extension of an adjacent water treatment plant, and a return of reclaimed land to public use as a recreational site with landscaped open space, sports facilities, and an extensive network of walking trails. As one part of this master plan, the client sought to create new facilities for the County Environmental Services Division—a building planned to provide fifty thousand square feet of space to house storm-water management, solid waste, water, and wastewater programs that Miller|Hull was commissioned to design in 1999.

Oriented along a north-south axis, this new building has been designed to underscore the scale and complexity of this imaginative restoration initiative. And although it is located so as to create a lookout over the site and take in the long views out over Puget Sound and to Mount Ranier, the building has also been planned to respond to this location by providing a twenty-foot overhang on the glazed west-facing facade and shading and an array of trees that protect it on the east. This emphasis on developing a design shaped by the environment has also created workspaces that are naturally lit and ventilated. In this context the choice of a concrete structure also provides thermal capacity that effectively tempers the climate within the building, and a series of vertical light wells that have been cut perpendicularly along the length of the building introduce daylight into the heart of the workspaces, help to induce airflow, and reduce the need for mechanical cooling. Also in response to its setting, the new Environmental Services Building has been kept long and low. The roof has been detailed to collect rainwater and deliver it by a system of dramatic scuppers to a bioswale, where it is treated prior to flowing into a system of infiltration ponds that extend through the site. This "rewriting of programming" integrates this new everyday service center into the reconstructed natural landscapes on the site and makes the building an educational device that helps to reveal natural systems to the community that it serves. By advancing integrative design into such a large-scale project, the architects have been able to assist in radically transforming formerly privately owned land and service buildings into distinctly public works.

These public works are not limited to the restoration and reuse of land beyond the city. The Bainbridge City Hall, a modest civic building that houses all of the facilities for local government in an island community in the Puget Sound, was built on the site of a former gas station and parking lot. Consequently it reclaims land at the heart of a community but at the same time assertively designates that land for public use. By studying the potential of this reclaimed site, the scheme also made it possible for the site to be used as a public green space through the week, a farmers market on weekends, and overflow parking for major events in the town. The building itself has been designed to encourage the overlapping of uses internally and detailed to make extensive use of recycled materials. It is clearly a new modern public building yet one that sits comfortably alongside its residential neighbours and creates an inspiring civic focus.

In 2000, Miller|Hull designed the Fisher Pavilion at Seattle Center—an impressive new urban room in the heart of Seattle. Prompted by an interest in creating a mix of indoor and outdoor spaces that would encourage new activities to enliven an existing public park, the pavilion was designed to provide fourteen thousand square feet of space that could accommodate exhibitions, receptions, celebrations, and public events while extending the landscape of the existing park. Initially appointed to rebuild an existing building on the site, the architect's idea of developing a new subterranean building beneath the designated site had the effect of doubling the new floor area. Tucked into an existing slope, the building creates a horseshoe of space that can be subdivided in different ways according to the needs of the various users and events. It opens up to a green in the park and an impressive public fountain beyond. The roof of the new building has been designed to provide a paved space at the upper level, which can be used as an additional outdoor display area and terrace while at the same time also serving as a forecourt for the existing Children's Theatre, which is alongside. This urban intervention transformed the need to create spaces for a diverse range of community activities by reinventing the site while responding to the wider context of a public landscape.

At a time when there is renewed interest in design and an urgent need to develop a sustainable approach to architecture and the construction of cities that does more than merely reflect fashion and the additive prescriptions of LEED certification, these new public works designed by Miller|Hull are of particular importance. They demonstrate how ideas developed for small projects that focus on the systemic can be made relevant in other strikingly different contexts. And while Miller|Hull had developed a wealth of ideas related to siting and the choice of materials, thoughtful construction, and inspired integration of systems to effectively define the private spaces of "the cabin," their expanding portfolio of work, detailed in this book, reveals other aspects of reality that have remained hidden. Miller|Hull's recent "comings and goings" across a wider community of designers also highlight new opportunities for architecture. The integration and visibility of building systems, energy, material, and landscape have been expanded with the successful and radical reworkings of different programs. Buildings are becoming landscape and the private room of the cabin exchanged for new public space. This recent work of Miller|Hull presents an alternative and obviously viable model for design that reveals fresh realities and inspires other patterns of architectural practice as we move into the twenty-first century.

Brian Carter

Notes

1 Renzo Piano, *The Process of Architecture* (London: 9H Gallery, 1987), 2.

2 Louis Kahn, *Louis Kahn: Conversations with Students* (New York: Princeton Architectural Press, 1998), 54.

3 Piano, *The Process of Architecture*, 2.

Brian Carter is an architect who worked in practice with Arup in London before taking up an academic appointment in the United States. The designer of a number of award-winning buildings in Europe, he is the author of several books including *Johnson Wax Administration Building and Research Tower* by Phaidon Press. His writings have been published in numerous professional journals—*The Architectural Review*, *AD*, *Architectural Record*, *DETAIL*, *The Journal of Architecture*, and *Casabella*—and he has curated a series of exhibitions about the work of Peter Rice, Eero Saarinen, Albert Kahn, and Charles and Ray Eames in Europe and North America. Brian Carter is currently professor and dean of the School of Architecture and Planning at the University at Buffalo, The State University of New York.

PUBLIC WORKS

SOUTH LAKE UNION DISCOVERY CENTER / Seattle, Washington

Overview

As with many urban sites, this building needed to accommodate and respond to many forces. The main goal was to create a building that could provide adaptable exhibition space for multiple new design projects in the emerging South Lake Union neighborhood, just north of the downtown Seattle urban core. In addition, the client loaned part of the site back to Seattle Parks and Recreation in order to preserve existing athletic fields, thereby establishing the buildable area along Westlake Avenue.

Design Vision

During programming discussions, the client stressed the importance of future flexibility (both in location and function), yet it also desired an iconic building that would serve its current functions well. To provide the most limitless solution, the team designed the building itself to be demountable and movable for future programmatic uses within the South Lake Union neighborhood. It also had a flexible interior space that could be modified easily over time. This was seen as the ultimate in sustainability, especially in the retail sector, which constantly evolves in response to current trends.

Execution

The final eleven thousand-square-foot structure is comprised of four-sided steel bents, paired together with bolted connections and free-spanning the interior gallery and exhibition space. The building envelope components are designed as prefabricated and modular assemblies, clad with durable metal wall and roof panels. Even the mechanical, electrical, and plumbing work is designed to be detachable when the building moves. Acting as a spine to the exhibition space, the wood-clad linear service bar component houses the support functions of the pavilion. To facilitate future transport, the dimensions of each separate module are designed to correspond to the size of a truck bed and the widths of neighborhood streets.

Opposite: Access ramps are hinged to meet grade, but more importantly, they allow the building to adjust to various site conditions at future locations.

Following spread: The wood roof structure cantilevers across the steel frame to provide a broad eave and protection from the elements.

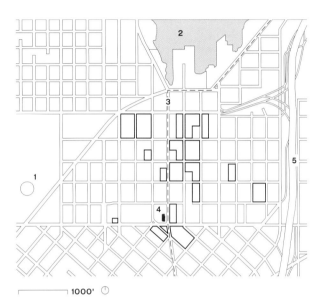

1000'

Above: The Discovery Center sits amid
a rapidly changing South Lake Union
neighborhood. Development projects
making use of the pavilion's amenities are
outlined in bold within the South Lake
Union Vicinity map. Key: (1) Seattle Center
Space Needle, (2) Lake Union, (3) trolley
line, (4) Discovery Center, (5) Interstate-5.

Opposite: South Lake Union Discovery
Center site plan and floor plan.
Key: (1) Denny Avenue, (2) Eastlake
Avenue, (3) main entry, (4) Seattle Parks
and Recreation athletic fields preserved by
the project, (5) service portion of the
building, (6) flexible exhibit space.

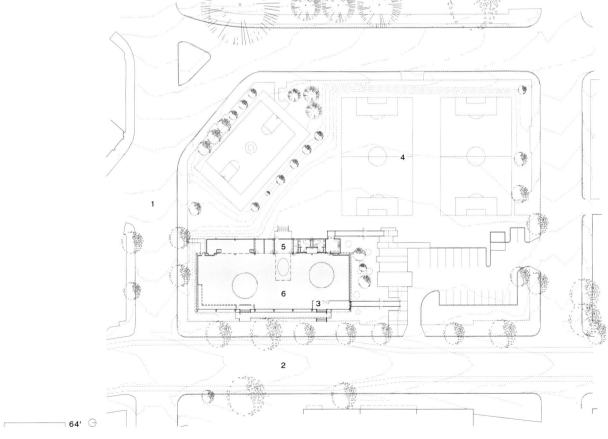

64'

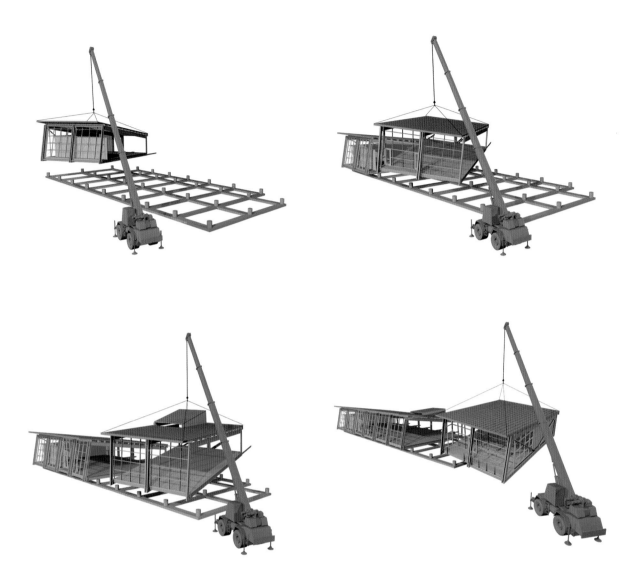

Above: Sequence of building module relocation.

Opposite, top: Building axonometric drawing showing repetition of structural bays and open floor plan for interior flexibility.

Opposite, bottom left: Detail of structural connections between bays, allowing for the building's disassembly. Key: (1) Steel frame, (2) concrete point load footings, (3) bolted connection between adjacent frames, (4) seam at roof structure, (5) seam at floor structure.

Opposite, bottom right: The wood ceiling deck and steel frame are expressed on both the interior and exterior, bringing the building's kit of parts into everyday view.

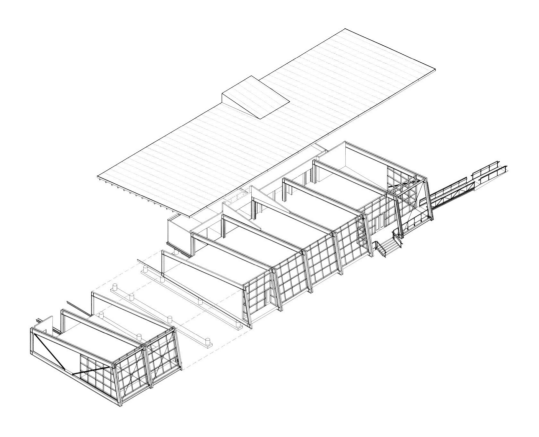

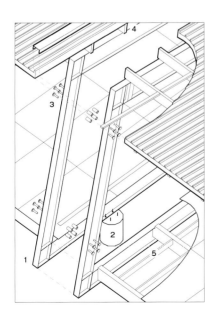

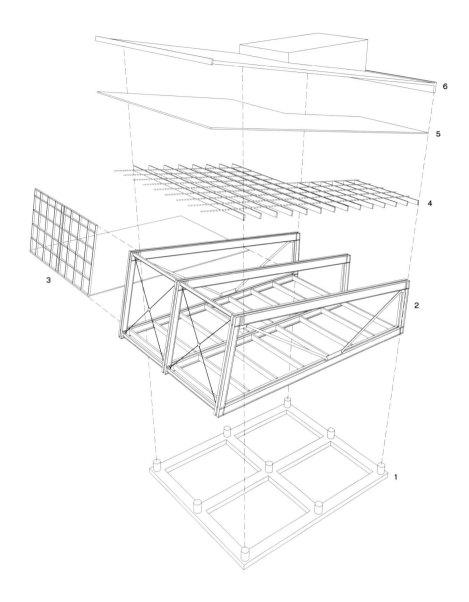

Above: The envelope can be broken
down into six basic components, all visible
in the expression of the building. Key:
(1) Point load footings, (2) steel frame,
(3) curtain wall, (4) wood joists,
(5) wood deck, (6) metal roof panels.

Opposite: Partial elevation showing one
structural bay, a width determined by
possible relocation routes and transport
vehicle.

Opposite: The Discovery Center's structural expression is at home in a neighborhood full of construction projects.

Above and left: A bioretention swale along the south and east sides of the parking lot manages stormwater for the site, precluding the need for an underground detention tank. These strategies decreased the peak water runoff rate by 44%, and the water runoff during a storm event is estimated to be only 37% of what a conventional building site would send into the city's stormwater system. The project served as a test case for the city of Seattle as it prepared to adopt a "green area ratio factor" requirement for the city's zoning code. To receive permit approval, a project must achieve a certain number of points based on the area of lawn, grass pavers, number and maturity of trees, and area of green roofs or walls, among other strategies.

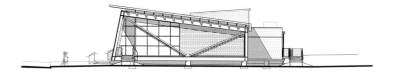

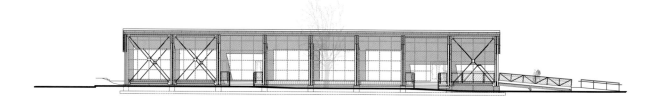

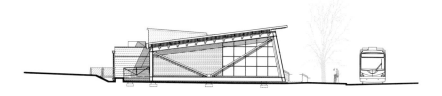

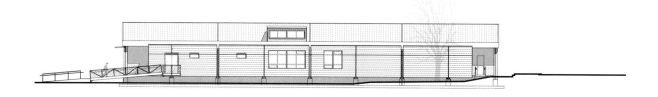

From top: North elevation, East elevation, South elevation, West elevation.

Opposite top: Street corner from above, at Denny Way and Westlake Avenue N.

Opposite, bottom: A linear north-south footprint maximized the site and provided ample exposure for the exhibits to be seen from Westlake Avenue N, which received a new trolley line connecting the South Lake Union area with downtown Seattle. The building's position on this corner gave it prominant retail frontage and anchored the urban edge along the sidewalk.

Following spread: This facade is fully glazed to bring in substantial natural light and to give maximum exposure to exhibits seen from the street.

TECHNOLOGY ACCESS FOUNDATION HEADQUARTERS
AND COMMUNITY LEARNING CENTER / White Center, Washington

Overview

The Technology Access Foundation (TAF) approached Miller|Hull to design a twenty-first-century learning facility. In addition to being a new headquarters for TAF operations, the building would also serve as a daytime recreational space for local families as well as a K–12 after-school community center. TAF was created with the mission of improving education among children of color by connecting them with technology tools and opportunities. In doing so, the Community Learning Center combines themes of sustainability, community, and technology into a single framework. In addition to Miller|Hull, the owner sought out Public Architecture, a nonprofit design firm working out of San Francisco. The firm consulted with the Miller|Hull design team on integrating salvaged materials, signage, and the overall design concepts.

Design Vision

Through a charrette process, the design team identified four primary design goals: (1) to minimize disruption on the existing park site; (2) to utilize the existing setting to set a mood throughout the building; (3) to create a unique destination and place for learning that reflects TAF's values and image; and (4) to use locally salvaged materials to reduce waste and connect to the local context.

Execution

The building program and its systems are organized by floor as a response to both security and efficiency. The lower floor opens up to the lake, with a direct connection from the building's outdoor patio to the park's trail system. Upper-floor offices and the flex spaces of the second floor are naturally ventilated for much of the year, with a radiant heating and radiant cooling slab system coupled with chilled beams available during peak cooling periods. The computer labs on the second floor are wrapped with a superinsulated exterior wall and are cooled with smaller decentralized air-conditioning units and underfloor systems to minimize ductwork. This allows the system to adjust to the specific needs of each classroom. All rainwater runoff from the roof is directed into planters that occupy some of the overhang spaces on the second floor and can be found adjacent to the lower-level courtyard.

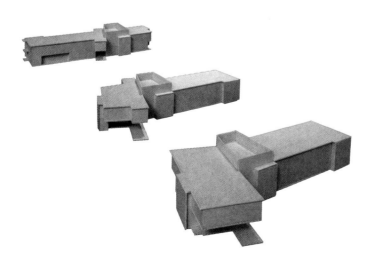

Above: The pedestrian bridge that links the existing parking lot to the proposed building provides an important symbolic threshold to anyone entering the facility. Once inside, the building features a series of cantilevers and overhangs provided by the larger building footprint of the upper levels, creating sheltered outdoor spaces and entries for the lower levels.

Left: A series of physical models were used by the team to study the building's form and organization.

Statistics*

1. 27.1 percent of White Center residents are foreign born.

2. Almost one-third of adult residents of White Center and Boulevard Park combined speak a language other than English at home.

3. About one in three residents of White Center and Boulevard Park do not earn a family-supporting income.

4. Child poverty levels are substantially higher in White Center and Boulevard Park than in King County as a whole.

5. White Center and Boulevard Park schools have among the lowest completion rates in King County. The completion rate for the Highline School District is less than two-thirds.

6. White Center and Boulevard Park schools are racially and culturally diverse, with no single racial or ethnic group in the majority: white (34 perent), Asian/Pacific Islander (33 percent), Hispanic/Latino (19 percent), Black/African American (12 percent), and American Indian/Alaska Native (2 percent).

7. Two-thirds of White Center and Boulevard Park elementary school students are enrolled in free- and reduced-lunch programs. For middle and high school students, the figure is 50 percent.

8. Residents of White Center and Boulevard Park are younger, on average, than the King County population as a whole. Approximately one in four residents of White Center and Boulevard Park is younger than eighteen.

*The statistics about the population of White Center are from U.S. Census Bureau data for 2000.

Opposite, top right: This diagram reflects the difference in scale between the capacity of the current program and the new facility.

Opposite, top left: This graph depicts the demographics of the local community that TAF will serve.

Opposite, middle: Vicinity map of White Center. Key: (1) Puget Sound, (2) Duwamish Waterway, (3) TAF site including Lake Garrett, (4) Evergreen High School, (5) Cascade Middle School, (6) Mt. View Elementary, (7) White Center Heights Elementary, (8) Shorewood Elementary.

Opposite, bottom: The TAF organization offers K–12 after-school programs that feature age-appropriate education, using technology as a tool to improve math literacy, critical thinking, problem solving, and information-processing skills.

Native American 1.3%
Multi-Racial / Other 6.6%

Hispanic 13%

White 15.4%

Asian / Pacific Islander 20.5%

African American 43.2%

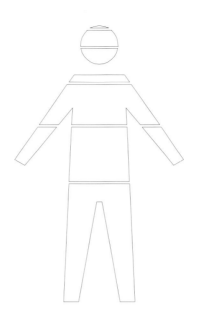

= 100 Students

Current Facility:
430 students enrolled, supports 825

New TAF Facility:
Support for 4,100 students

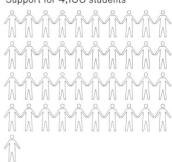

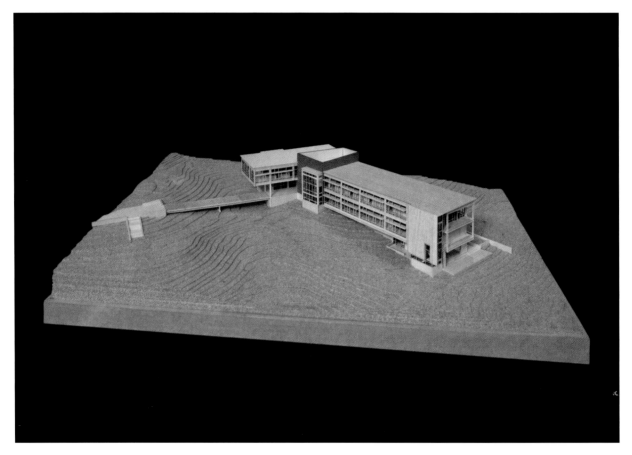

Top: The site located at the 13-acre
Lakewood Park is composed
of a series of meadows, tree groves,
and a small lake linked with meandering,
paved trails.

Bottom: Site model showing
the building's position in the park's
topography.

200'

Left: A study sketch of the entry
pedestrian bridge.

Right: As shown in this site plan,
the main building is placed deep within
the park to benefit from an existing grove
of trees and views of the lake, while the
existing rolling topography of the park
is preserved. (1) Technology Access
Foundation Community Learning Center,
(2) Lake Garrett, (3) Adjacent housing,
(4) Pedestrian bridge to main entry,
(5) Rainwater runoff collected from the
building and infiltrated through the
proposed raingarden.

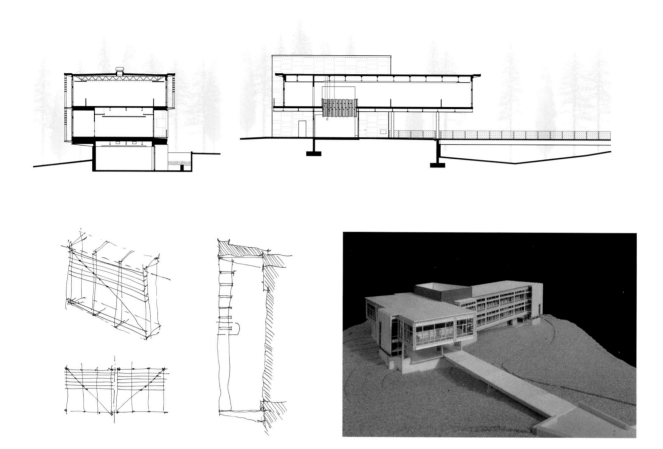

Top: In these typical building sections, large program elements are located on upper floors to create sheltering overhangs and minimize the building footprint.

Bottom left: The sun-shading system is made from off-the-shelf components and is held away from the exterior facade to allow operable windows to pivot into the space created between the building and the sunshades. This protects the interior from solar gain when the building is in full natural-ventilation mode.

Bottom right: The building expression derives from a desire for the building to appear as light and airy as possible. The steel frame is exposed on the exterior and interior, forming a suspended box infilled with glass.

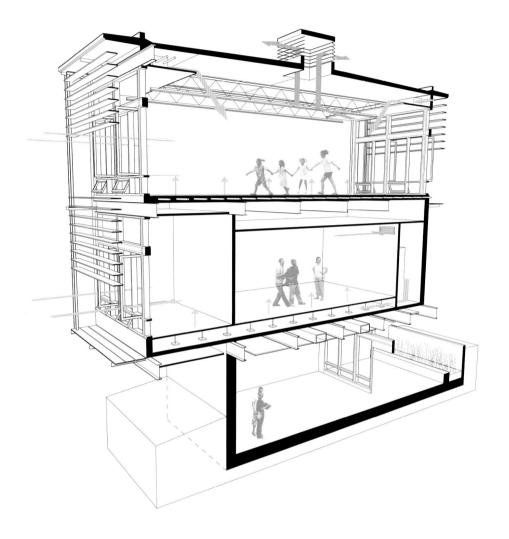

Above: The program organization facilitated a unique mechanical system approach. Upper-floor offices and the flex spaces (which have lower heating and cooling loads) are naturally ventilated for much of the year and include a radiant heating and cooling slab system. Perimeter chilled beams are useful during peak cooling periods and in spaces that are more susceptible to solar gain. Larger computer labs (which typically have higher mechanical loads and require dedicated cooling for equipment) on the second floor are wrapped with a superinsulated exterior wall and are cooled with smaller decentralized air-conditioning units and underfloor systems to minimize ductwork. Also visible in this section is the raingarden that collects the building's rainwater runoff and becomes a natural feature adjacent to the lower-level multipurpose room and covered patio.

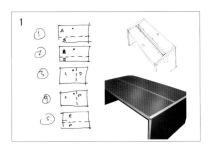

Salvaged materials are used for enclosure, exterior cladding, interior finishes, and one-of-a-kind art installations throughout the building. These materials include highway signs, cabinet fronts, fire hoses, and scrap-metal offcuts. The design team developed a "narrative approach" to sourcing and designing with this salvaged material. These narratives were used by the design team and by members of the community to visualize, understand, and source appropriate salvaged material. A variety of approaches were developed, and some have even been prototyped in smaller installations at TAF's smaller branch offices.

(1) Nationwide, thousands of solid-core doors are thrown away in renovations. The team developed a simple two-sided desk design for TAF employees made entirely of salvaged solid-core doors that were milled onsite. Waste was minimized by strategic use of most of the door material: ten doors create three double-sided workstations.

(2) Using damaged Seattle Fire Department supply hose, the design team developed a wood-framed partition wall that also serves as an acoustic partition. Special lap details were developed to hang the hose, which is applied much like horizontal siding to the bare stud framing, negating the need for taping, painting, or otherwise finishing the wall surface.

(3) Seattle bus stops use decorative glass panels to form a weather enclosure. When these panels are damaged or vandalized, they are replaced and the removed panels are typically thrown away. Using some of these salvaged standard-dimension panels, the TAF design team created lighted kids' cubbies that are located in each classroom of the TAF building.

(4) Heavy timber beams pulled from a housing project demolition site were sorted and stored for future use as pedestrian bridge decking at the TAF project. This heavy material considerably reduced the size of the bridge structure required for a more conventional system.

(5) Often large aluminum sheet metal is damaged during transport, and some metal shops are forced to buy larger material than can be handled in their machinery. As a result, new sheet metal is wasted and returned to the recycling stream, requiring more energy to melt it down and reform it into new materials. The TAF building uses these rough offcuts as a shingle-style wall covering, forming the outer protective layer in a rainscreen wall system that covers the building's core.

(6) The ScrapHouse, completed by associate firm Public Architecture, is a demonstration single-family house constructed entirely from salvaged materials. Much of the impetus for the use of salvaged materials in the TAF facility came from MillerHull's working relationship with Public Architecture.

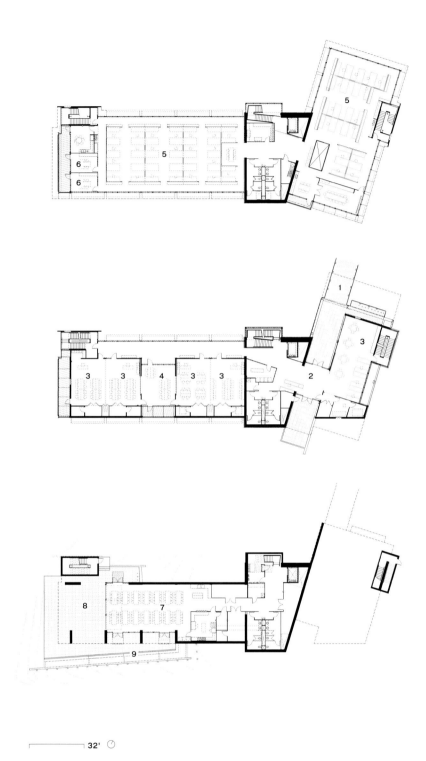

32'

Above, from top: Second floor,
first floor, and lower floorplans.
Key: (1) Pedestrian bridge, (2) main lobby,
(3) computer training labs, (4) tutoring
spaces, (5) open offices, (6) conference
room, (7) community room, (8) outdoor
courtyard, (9) raingardens.

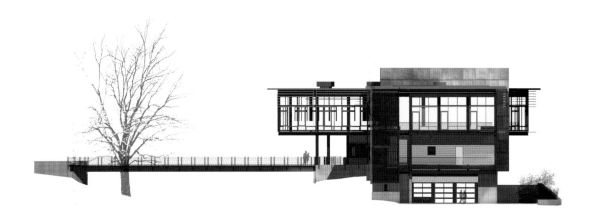

North elevation
South elevation

East elevation
West elevation

The building skin is as transparent as
possible, with sun shading to control
heat gain and glare. The sun shade
design later evolved to become more
industrially scaled to also function as
window washing platforms. Egress
stairs, one visible at the left of the
image, are unconditioned but enclosed
with metal grating. This reduces the
mechanical loads for the building yet
allows weather protection and
ventilation year-round.

The building form was thought of as being "surgically inserted" into the existing park topography. This was expressed by allowing the building to meet the site cleanly, without additive landscaping obscuring the concrete stem walls at their base. Deep overhangs at the south provide summer sun protection for the exterior spaces, while allowing low winter sun to penetrate the building.

WILSONVILLE WATER TREATMENT PLANT / Wilsonville, Oregon

Overview

Situated on a prominent knoll above the picturesque Willamette River, the water treatment plant was originally designed by a large design-build company. It was conceived as a series of separate equipment buildings that would extract water from the river and purify it into drinking water for the local community. The initial layout spread process buildings over the entire site and surrounded the property with chain link fence. Landscape architects and an architect were hired to accept this configuration and provide screening and "beautification." When the plan met with disappointment from the residential neighborhoods surrounding the site, the client started over and hired Miller|Hull.

Design Vision

To begin, the Miller|Hull team researched the process of water purification—from extraction, sedimentation, filtration, ozonation, and polishing to clear-water storage, pressurization, and distribution. The process turned out to be quite sequential and linear, with specific building elements housing particular steps in the treatment process. The team began to realize that there were parallels between the plant's treatment process and nature's typical filtration process. The critical question was, if one were to draw a north-south line through the center of the site, could one side accommodate plant needs (and future growth), leaving the other side available for public amenities? Aside from clear-water storage, which would be stored underground, this diagram seemed to work.

Execution

The north-south line that bisects the site is manifested as an 800-foot concrete and stone garden wall. It provides a separation device between the secure water treatment plant and a public park and stream. The garden wall also serves as a connector for a series of building elevations that house the public works functions beyond. It acts as the circulation element for visitors to learn about the facility: window portals provide views through the garden wall and into the process spaces, while interpretive panels explain the piping, pumps, filters, and operating functions. The top of the wall stays constant as the site drops to the riverbank, emphasizing gravity's role in the natural process and illustrating the natural slope down to the river. The visitor's experience at the water treatment plant culminates in a river-view lookout via a stream and path that explains nature's method of water purification.

Opposite: The still water surrounding the meeting room allows sedimentation to occur and provides a calm backdrop for events held in the space.

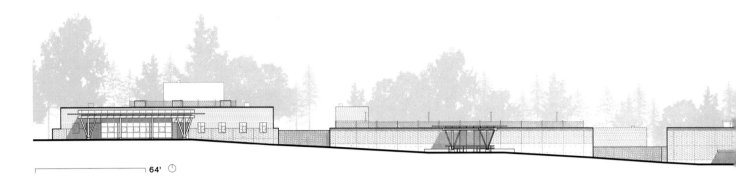

64'

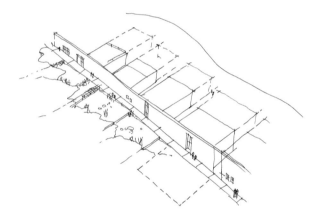

Above: An early concept sketch of the garden wall with plant facilities on one side and landscaped public space on the other. Future areas for expansion of the plant's capacity are dashed in on the aerial sketch.

Top: Site elevation and site photograph montage showing the linear sequence of the plant facilities and public park. It became apparent during the research phase that the water purification process at the Wilsonville Water Treatment Plant mimics the earth's natural purification process. As a parallel experience along this wall, water moves through plant materials and rocky falls mimicking nature's own filtration process on the way to the Willamette River.

Opposite: Site plan of the facility. Dashed lines show future expansion. Key: (1) Public meeting room, (2) Administration Building, (3) chemical storage, (4) ozone generation, (5) sedimentation, (6) ozonation, (7) picnic shelter, (8) filtration, (9) public park, (10) high service pump station, (11) below grade clear water storage, (12) raw water pump station, (13) view point, (14) Willamette River.

Following spread: View looking north along the garden wall, the public park and trail that cover the below-grade clean water reservoir.

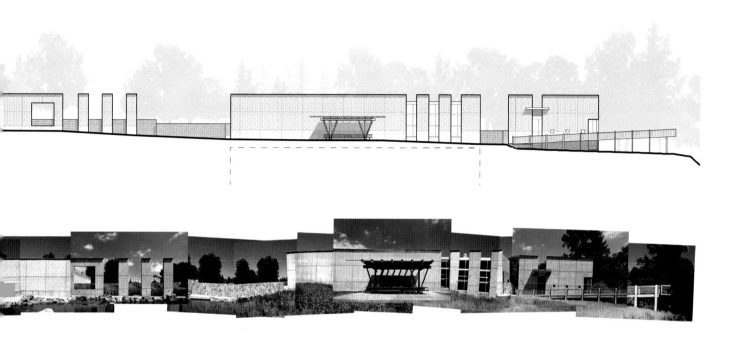

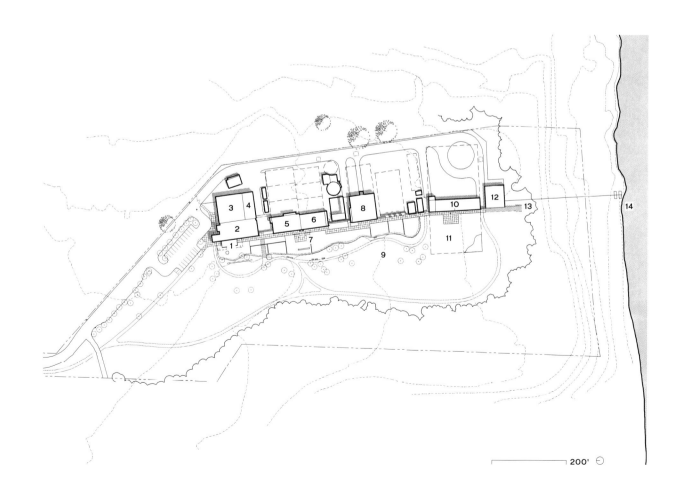

200' ⊖

Opposite and above: Technology within the plant mimics nature's filtration processes. In nature, when water cascades over falls, it is aerated and filtered. When this happens while water is exposed to sunlight, ozonation occurs, allowing bacteria and microbes to be broken down by UV light. To purify water at this facility, each of these stages are addressed in various plant buildings.

Top: The board-form concrete wall visible along the path provides an anchor for all the brick-enclosed plant facilities behind the wall. The water on the right of the wall flows on its natural course to the river.

Bottom: The water treatment tanks are visible to the public.

Above: Openings in the concrete walls allow visitors to see all the equipment required to purify, pressurize, and pump the water back to the city. Accompanying the openings in the wall are interpretative panels describing these processes to visitors. The plant was laid out so that future capacity could be added to the facility in its current configuration behind the garden wall.

Above left: A public meeting room attaches to the wall and sits in the pond.

Above, top right: Because of the architecture and native landscaping—atypical for water treatment plants—the facility has become an amenity for the surrounding residential neighborhoods in the form of a public park and access to the river.

Above, bottom right: Interior of public meeting room at the facility looking out to the surrounding landscape.

Opposite top: In the public park and stream side of the facility, two shelters attached to the wall contain tables long enough for student groups and other visitors to gather. They are visible under the wood canopies.

Opposite bottom: Areas of still water allow sedimentation to occur: heavier solid particles settle to the bottom, and clearer water flows beyond. As in nature, this stage in the treatment is part of the plant's process.

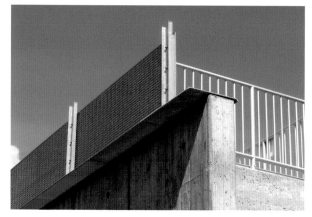

Above top: The long concrete and stone garden wall not only acts as a visual screen between the public park, it also serves as a security wall preventing unauthorized access to the city's supply of drinking water.

Above left: The interpretive sidewalk extends as an elevated promenade leading to a picturesque view of the Willamette River and to public shoreline access.

Above right: The moist climate conditions in the Pacific Northwest will deteriorate concrete walls if they are not properly protected at the top. Here, a steel plate is used as a consistent drip detail to provide protection and create a shadow line accentuating the concrete forms.

Opposite: Grasses and rocks provide drought tolerant landscaping for the region's dry summers.

Opposite, top: The water treatment
plant buildings and the river outfall.

Opposite, bottom right: The 800-foot
concrete and stone wall acts as both
a garden wall and a durable construction
for the treatment facility.

Opposite, bottom left: A view through
the garden wall.

Above: The landscaping used at the
treatment plant and park is native and
provides a habitat corridor along the
Willamette River.

Following spread: A concrete facility
visible beyond the plant walls provided
locally harvested material for the project.

TILLAMOOK FOREST INTERPRETIVE CENTER / Tillamook, Oregon

Overview

Four massive fires between 1933 and 1951 swept through the original forest, leaving behind a stark, blackened landscape. Oregonians' response to this disaster led to the establishment and stewardship of the Tillamook State Forest. This interpretive center was designed to explain the history, recreation, and forest practices of the 355,000-acre Tillamook Forest to provide a sustainable range of social, environmental, and economic benefits to the people of Oregon. The center focuses on the story of the "Tillamook burn," a devastating forest fire that obliterated more than 350,000 acres of forest. A massive two-decade reforestation effort ensued. The reforestation brought back the forest, but the lack of tree species diversity created a monoculture that the Forestry Department has since been correcting by planting new species, creating snags for habitat and openings in the tree canopy. The center is situated within an area of forest diversification, so the interpretive elements that tell the story of the restoration efforts are both inside and outside.

Design Vision

The interpretive nature of this building's function and the desire to weave the building into the forest led to a linear solution. The building takes its form from the historical skid that is a long-level, partially covered platform for moving and sawing timber. In this case the skid becomes the arrival point. A bridge that spans across the Wilson River connects the interpretive center to campgrounds and trails. The building entry spans a pond created by roof stormwater runoff. The pond is used as a storage area for water, for the building's fire sprinklers, for an alternative source for refilling fire engines, for flushing toilets, and for what little mechanical cooling of the building is required. The main event is the interpretive exhibition space, which doubles as the lobby and occupies one long continuous space.

Execution

The building was conceived and executed in a way that tells the story of wood construction. Throughout framing and layers of finish are expressed and wood products are the primary finish material. The structural system and windows consist of certified wood and engineered wood products from the Oregon region. Slung alongside the skid exhibition hall space is a secondary building of the same form that houses classrooms, the gift shop, administration spaces, and the theater, as well as restrooms and mechanical rooms.

Opposite: Main entry at dusk.

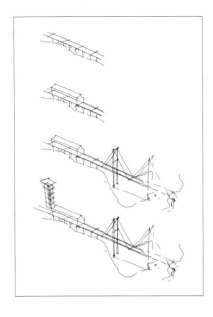

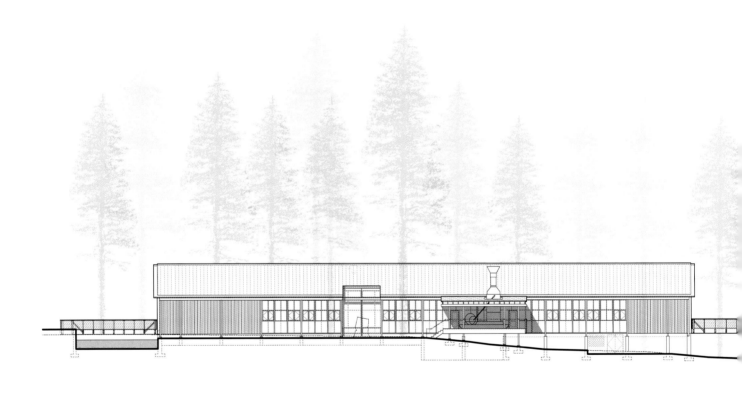

Top left: The skid structure is erected first and becomes the armature for organizing the building elements. The interpretive lobby is then added to the platform, followed by the pedestrian bridge and interpretive lookout tower.

Top right: Historic photograph of early logging operations on the platform structure known as a "skid." A skid is a long, level, partially covered platform for moving and sawing lumber.

Bottom: East elevation including the fire protection pond, "nurse stump" and "steam donkey" exhibits, and pedestrian bridge over Wilson River.

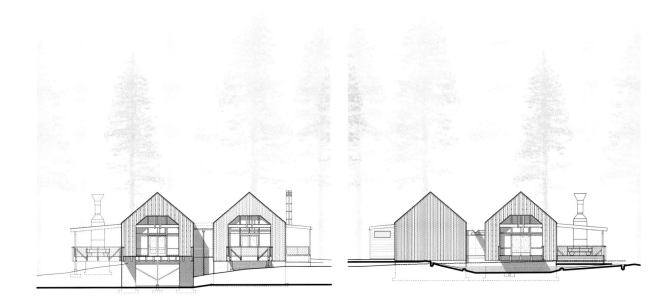

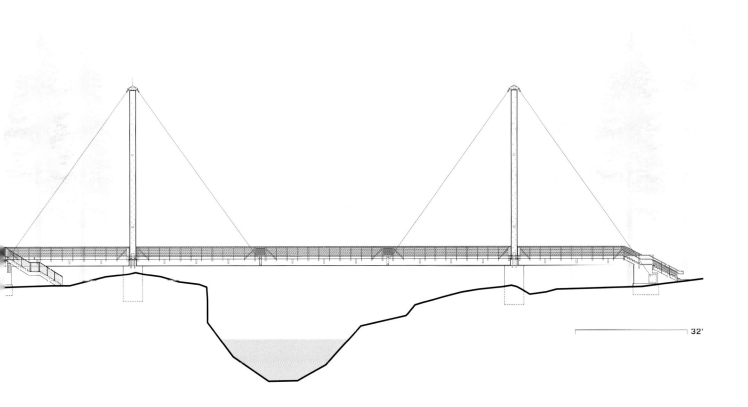

Above: North and South elevations.

32'

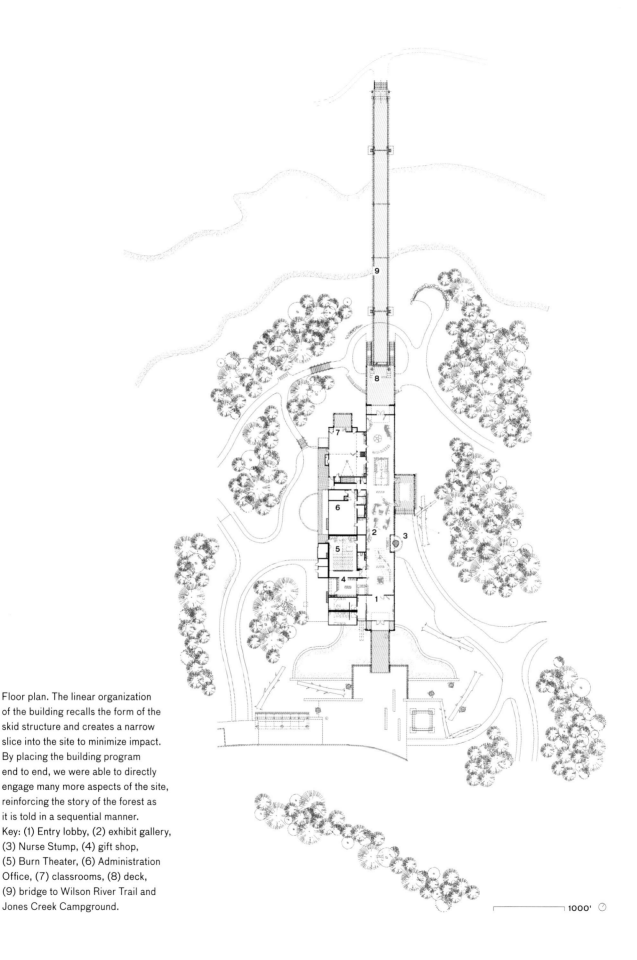

Floor plan. The linear organization
of the building recalls the form of the
skid structure and creates a narrow
slice into the site to minimize impact.
By placing the building program
end to end, we were able to directly
engage many more aspects of the site,
reinforcing the story of the forest as
it is told in a sequential manner.
Key: (1) Entry lobby, (2) exhibit gallery,
(3) Nurse Stump, (4) gift shop,
(5) Burn Theater, (6) Administration
Office, (7) classrooms, (8) deck,
(9) bridge to Wilson River Trail and
Jones Creek Campground.

1000'

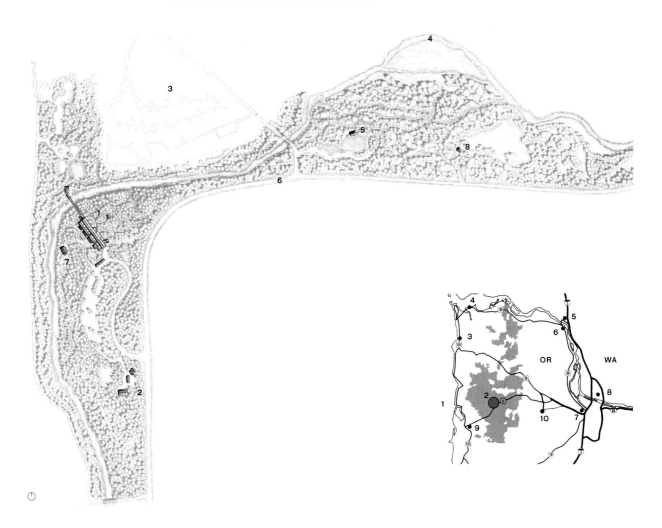

Above: Site plan. Key: (1) Interpretive
Center, (2) caretaker/maintenance,
(3) Jones Creek Campground, (4) Jones
Creek (5) day use area, (6) Highway-6,
(7) Wilson River, (8) Smith Homestead.

Above inset: Vicinity map outlining the
Interpretive Center and landmarks. Key.
(1) Pacific Ocean, (2) Tillamook Forest
Interpretive Center, (3) Seaside, OR,
(4) Astoria, OR, (5) Longview, WA,
(6) Rainier, OR, (7) Portland, OR,
(8) Vancouver, WA, (9) Tillamook, OR,
(10) Forest Grove, OR.

Left: Miller|Hull also designed the
shelter at the Smith Homestead site for
the Oregon Department of Forestry. It is
a year-round outdoor learning center.

Left: View from pedestrian bridge to the interpretive lobby. The gable form on the right houses the classroom.
Top right: Four major forest fires burned through thisi area from 1933 to 1951 covering a total of 355,000 acres.
Middle right: Original fire watch tower.
Bottom right: As an interpretive element a reconstructed fire watch tower allows visitors to experience what the life of a forest ranger is like. Although this tower is not used for spotting fires, as with the original, it provides exceptional territorial views.

Opposite, top: The building highlights typical wood construction. The siding is typical board and batten, but at the covered entry the battens are removed, which reveals the framing and creates a lantern effect.

Opposite, bottom: The east elevation of the building is glazed the entire length of the interpretive lobby.

Top left: The building itself highlights the use of sustainable wood products throughout and is part of the interpretive experience. By providing a slatted wood ceiling reminiscent of skip sheathing, the acoustic battens and electrical lines can be concealed while still expressing the wood construction.

Top right: The double king post for the roof truss allows the sprinkler line to run at the ridge and feed down in between the rafters.

Bottom: Opposite the window wall is an educational mural by Aldrich Pears Interpretive Design that runs the length of the solid wall. Doors to the classrooms are concealed within the mural.

Opposite: A significant site feature is the nurse stump. Rather than place the building outside the stump, it was sited so as to engage it and make it the focus of one of the interpretive displays.

Top: The pedestrian bridge glu-lam beams
were not sized for the span but had to be
heavy enough to dampen the potential for
resonant oscillation as a result of wind.

Bottom: An outdoor exhibit area highlights
a steam donkey, used to maneuver logs
onto train cars, that was abandoned in the
forest after a 1932 fire.

Top left: A metal silo and auger system feed the pellets to the high-efficiency boilers. The ash is reintroduced into the forest.

Top middle: The mechanical fuel source is wood pellets, which are a by-product of the forest industry and are carbon-neutral.

Top right and bottom: The fire protection rainwater pond holds 65,000 gallons of water. It is used for supplementing the building's sprinkler systems, for flushing toilets, and for mechanical cooling.

Above: Using the long level platform as
the basis for programmatic organization,
as well as construction, allowed the
building to float above the natural grade
and minimized the impact of the site.

Opposite: Weyerhaeuser donated
the engineering and materials for the
pedestrian bridge that connects the
center to the trails on the fifty-acre site.
Construction began with the insertion
of the bridge and progressed by backing
out through the forest. This approach
minimized environmental impact to the site.

PIERCE COUNTY ENVIRONMENTAL SERVICES BUILDING /

University Place, Washington

Overview

Pierce County, in western Washington state, had long recognized the potential for converting this depleted gravel quarry to a public amenity; and in 1992 the county acquired the more than 700 acres of spent quarry on the southeast edge of the Puget Sound for the expansion of a wastewater treatment facility. The master plan for the site, developed by Seattle-based architectural firm Arai Jackson, won a National Planning Award. It transformed the previous raw quarry into a diverse array of community amenities, including a championship-level golf course, playfields and park lands (all built over manufactured soils irrigated with treated wastewater), a boat launch, an environmental education center, an arboretum, and a production nursery, as well as beaches, docks, and miles of public trails and pathways. County government functions on site include the wastewatwer treatment plant, administrative offices building, and maintenance services building. The first building to be built from the master plan is the 50,000-square-foot administrative offices for Environmental Services for Pierce County.

Design Vision

For the team, the question became: how do we set the tone for the forthcoming large-scale public amenity, on a dramatic site, with an office building? The answer came from the commitment displayed by the county's engineers and planners to the environment. The clients and design team worked together to push the limits to promote low-impact development and solid-waste recycling, while incorporating advanced wastewater technologies such as engineered biosolids and cogeneration.

Another tone-setting opportunity was the county's desire to build a much needed conference facility as part of the project. Miller|Hull, with the help of AldrichPears exhibit design, decided to capitalize on this opportunity by creating an "interpretive lobby," using the queuing requirements of the conference facility as a reason to oversize the lobby. This allowed the lobby to house some exhibits showing off the good work being done by the county's environmental services departments.

Opposite: A translucent panel baffle system was developed in conjunction with the Seattle Daylighting lab to bring diffuse natural light into the open office environment that also controls glare at workstations.

To take advantage of the site's truly spectacular views of the Puget Sound and the Cascade range (including Mount Rainier), the building orientation is north-south, with overhangs and sunscreens providing shading. The footprint has been kept narrow, allowing all workstations to be located within ten meters of exterior glazing. With the addition of skylights, every desk benefits from natural light. The building diagram began with the desire to separate public and private zones, knowing that the rentable meeting rooms and the interpretive lobby would be active, vibrant spaces—and therefore potentially disruptive to the office work also taking place. For that reason the solid-block core element was deliberately stretched east and west to provide that buffer and a soft separation of departments.

Execution

Concrete was the obvious choice for the primary building material, not only because of the nature of the site material but because the fabric energy storage—that is, the ability of concrete to absorb and store heat—combined with nighttime ventilation reduced the energy demand on the building. The design team developed a concept that integrated mechanical and structural goals: staggered concrete cores along with concrete structural columns and beams would define an open plan and extensively glazed exterior envelope.

During the day, sunlight hits the concrete walls through adjacent skylights. The sun's heat supplemented with mechanically delivered heat is absorbed by the concrete structure, which provides a more even and efficient heat. To contrast with summer conditions, a "night flush" sends cool air throughout the building. The concrete cores keep the building cooler and reduce the need for mechanically cooled air in warmer months. During the workday, air is delivered via a raised access floor directly at "human height," thereby reducing the over-cooling or over-heating required when delivering forced air from tall ceilings high above the occupied zone. Taller ceilings, however, brought in more natural daylight, creating a more desirable working environment. In fact, since the building's completion, staff turnover and absenteeism has declined greatly. Now the county can boast of a workspace that is as healthy as the goals it strives to promote.

Top: The building is situated at the edge of the bluff overlooking the Puget Sound below, with Mount Rainier in the background.

Bottom left: Rainwater is made visible by diverting it to a roof scupper supported by a cantilevered beam. It then drops into a large catchment that channels water into a raingarden.

Bottom right: View west from the wetland boardwalk to the Puget Sound.

Images 1–6: The Steilacoom aggregate mine and processing site on the Puget Sound, south of Tacoma, was one of the largest sand and gravel operations in the United States. It was worked for more than a hundred years, heavily transforming the local topography. The property also contains the tidal estuary of Chambers Bay, the heavily treed Chambers Creek Canyon, two miles of Puget Sound frontage, miles of creek frontage, and a variety of county services and operations.

Image 7: The site includes a championship-level golf course, which opened for play in 2007 and was built over manufactured soils and irrigated with treated wastewater. The course was designed by Robert Treny Jones II and is already recognized as one of the top courses in the world.

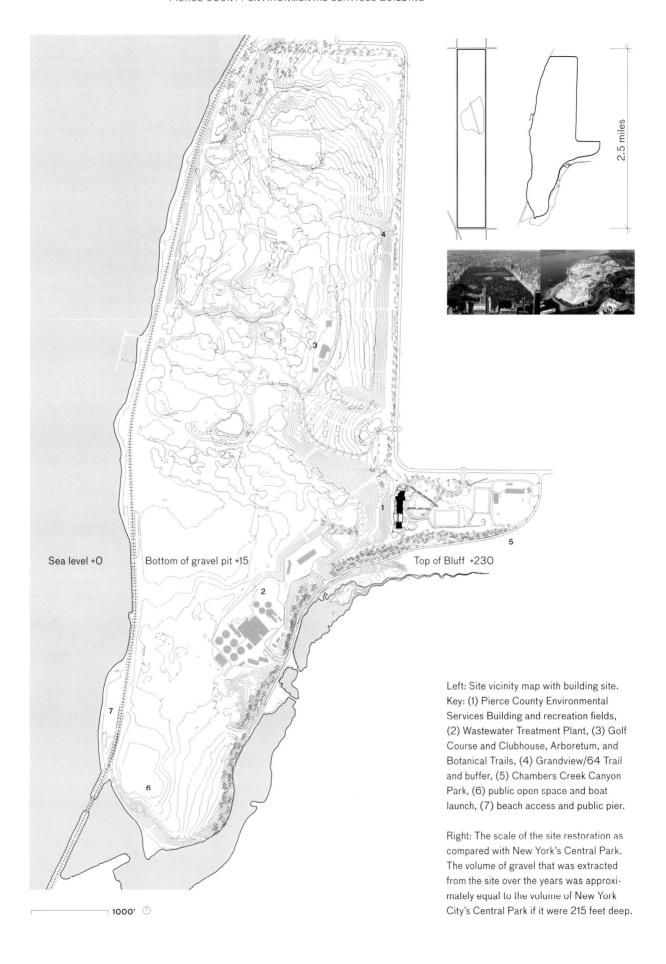

2.5 miles

Sea level +0   Bottom of gravel pit +15   Top of Bluff +230

1000'

Left: Site vicinity map with building site.
Key: (1) Pierce County Environmental
Services Building and recreation fields,
(2) Wastewater Treatment Plant, (3) Golf
Course and Clubhouse, Arboretum, and
Botanical Trails, (4) Grandview/64 Trail
and buffer, (5) Chambers Creek Canyon
Park, (6) public open space and boat
launch, (7) beach access and public pier.

Right: The scale of the site restoration as
compared with New York's Central Park.
The volume of gravel that was extracted
from the site over the years was approximately equal to the volume of New York
City's Central Park if it were 215 feet deep.

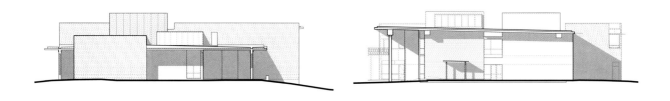

From top: West elevation, East elevation,
North elevation, South elevation

Opposite, top: Upper floor plan.
Key:(1) Open office, (2) private offices
and conference rooms, (3) Core:
workroom, kitchen, bathrooms,
mechanical/electrical/IT server rooms,
and storage

Opposite, middle: Ground floor plan.
Key: (1) Open office, (2) Private offices
and conference rooms, (3) Core:
workrooms, bathrooms, mechanical/
electrical room, (4) Interpretive Lobby,
(5) multipurpose room, (6) kitchens,
(7) training, (8) storage, (9) wellness
room.

Opposite, bottom: Conceptual plan
diagram showing core elements, light
pockets, and the lobby (in red).

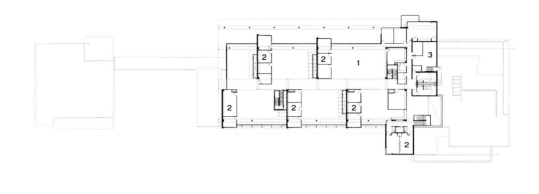

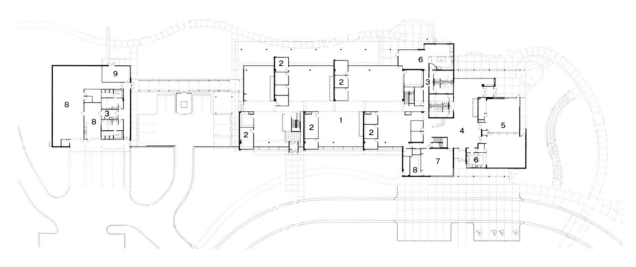

64'

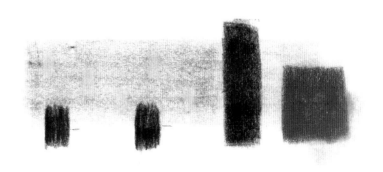

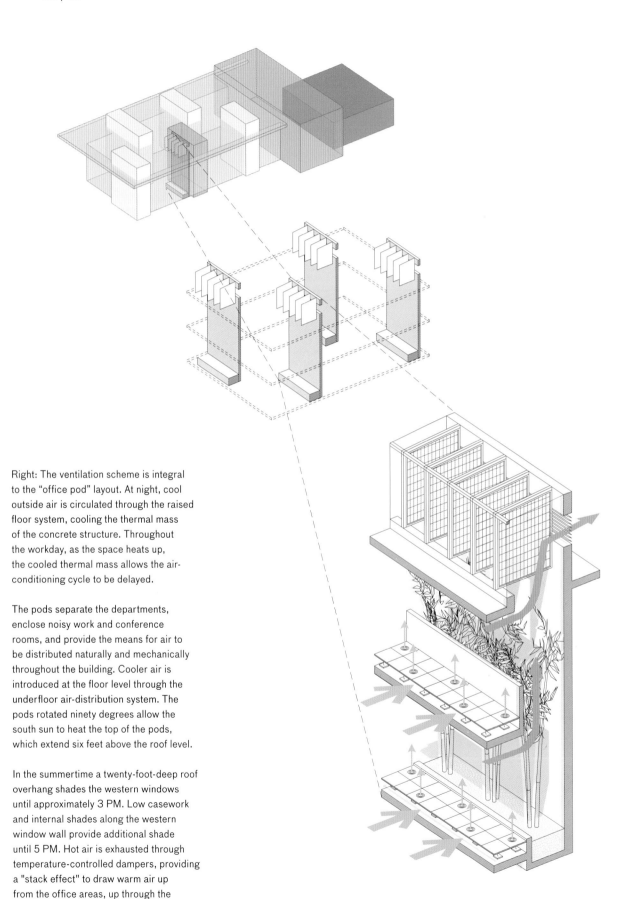

Right: The ventilation scheme is integral to the "office pod" layout. At night, cool outside air is circulated through the raised floor system, cooling the thermal mass of the concrete structure. Throughout the workday, as the space heats up, the cooled thermal mass allows the air-conditioning cycle to be delayed.

The pods separate the departments, enclose noisy work and conference rooms, and provide the means for air to be distributed naturally and mechanically throughout the building. Cooler air is introduced at the floor level through the underfloor air-distribution system. The pods rotated ninety degrees allow the south sun to heat the top of the pods, which extend six feet above the roof level.

In the summertime a twenty-foot-deep roof overhang shades the western windows until approximately 3 PM. Low casework and internal shades along the western window wall provide additional shade until 5 PM. Hot air is exhausted through temperature-controlled dampers, providing a "stack effect" to draw warm air up from the office areas, up through the pod chimneys, and out.

Left: The employee stair connecting
the first and second floor is illuminated
with natural light.

Top right: The transparency of the building
allows a line of sight through to the water
view beyond.

Bottom right: The open office floor plan
allows for a better working environment
with abundant natural light. The concrete
wall organizes the enclosed program areas
and provides the surface that channels
the natural light from the skylights above.

Above: The highly modulated western
facade with deep overhang allows for
views to Puget Sound from both floors
and provides sun protection.

Opposite: The eastern facade shading
strategy employs a vegetative sunscreen
of poplars aligned with the building's
structural bay and open metal grate
sunscreens in an "egg crate" configuration.

Left, top and bottom: The open bay between the end of the building and the support structure to the south allows for expansion for more of the office pod/open office concept as the department grows.

Right: Strategically placed window openings with deep overhangs provide daylight and framed views from the conference room in the solid core volume.

Top left: Not only are the conference rooms booked months in advance, but the events taking place at the Pierce County Environmental Services Building go beyond what was initially envisioned. Surprisingly, this government office building for the Department of Public Works—funded by sewer utility fees and located on the rim of an old gravel mining operation—books nearly every summer weekend for wedding receptions.

Middle left: Interpretive signage explains the stormwater treatment on site.

Bottom left: In order to encourage people to think about how what they throw away has an impact on the environment, the "Tower of Trash" exhibit in the lobby demonstrates the volume of solid waste generated by one person per year.

Right: By taking advantage of the over-sized lobby, exhibits that describe the sustainable practices of the county are incorporated into the queuing area for the conference facility.

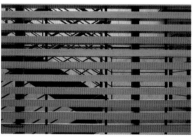

Above: The Lobby is articulated through
layers of transparency, translucency,
screens, and solids that define its volume.
The main stair is lit with translucent panels
that are apparent as one approaches the
main entry. It provides natural light during
the day and acts as a lit beacon at night.

Above: A simple palette of concrete, steel, and douglas fir are employed throughout. The vertical wood slat wall around the stair defines it while still revealing the function and the occupants as they use it.

Following spread: Native madrona trees anchor the northwest corner and provide a foreground to western views of Puget Sound from the building.

KITSAP COUNTY ADMINISTRATION BUILDING / Port Orchard, Washington

Overview

The initial inspiration for the Kitsap County Administration Building was derived from studying how Renzo Piano's studio in Italy and Arthur Erickson's Graham House in British Columbia navigated the sloped terrain. We were determined to turn this steep hillside site into an asset that capitalizes on the views and natural light, turning what could have been a rather ordinary office building into a dynamic building that creates a civic crossroads in downtown Port Orchard, Washington. By placing the main entrance on Division Street, across from the main entry to the Courthouse, we were able to link the front doors of the Courthouse, the Public Works Building, and the new Administration Building to create a civic presence on that corner. The lower floors of the 67,850-square-foot building are terraced into the 55-foot hillside, responding more informally and blending into a natural, land-scaped setting.

Design Vision

The building is conceived as a series of stepped terraces that spiral away from the central vertical circulation. The elevators are the lynchpin around which the stairs and floor levels are arranged. Building on what we learned from the Pierce County Environmental Services Building, we wanted to find a way to house the mechanical equipment in a central core and shield it from public view.

Execution

The site allows for a gracious terracing of office spaces and reduces the scale of the building, which allows it to respect the neighboring houses while maintaining a civic presence. Within the open offices, the incorporation of skylights at the rear of the spaces allows natural light into spaces deep within the building, and contributes toward the overall building cooling. Underfloor air distribution was used in this project, again based on our success with the Pierce County Environmental Services Building. We capitalized on the thermal mass of concrete to naturally cool the building. In this case, however, instead of using "pods" to exhaust the warm air through "chimneys," we chose to use the sky-lit corridors on each terrace floor for return air that is ducted to the heat recovery system in the mechanical penthouse.

Opposite: The main stair viewed from the north begins outside and continues through four levels of the building, connecting to grade fifty-five feet above.

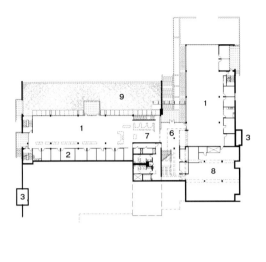

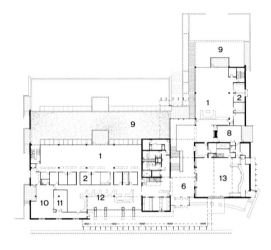

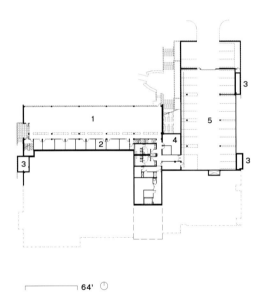

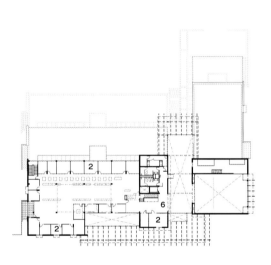

64'

Clockwise from bottom left:
Plans for first, second, third, and fourth
floors. Key: (1) Open office, (2) enclosed
offices and conference rooms, (3) cistern,
(4) wellness room, (5) parking,
(6) lobby, (7) Department of Community
Development Permit Area, (8) storage,
(9) green roof, (10) election/training
room, (11) ballot counting area,
(12) public counter, (13) commissioner's
chamber.

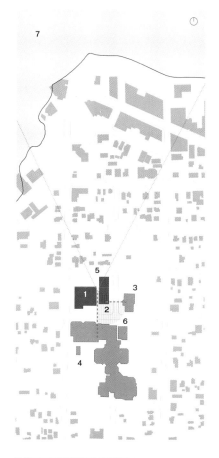

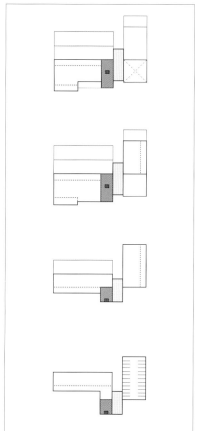

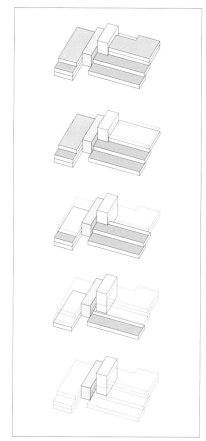

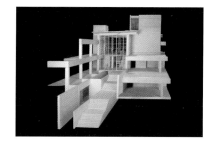

Top left: Vicinity map showing civic corner and view cone from main stair. Key: (1) Kitsap County Administration Building, (2) new plaza, (3) Public Works, (4) County Courthouse, (5) Elevation ninety-eight feet above sea level, (6) Elevation 153 feet above sea level, (7) Port Orchard Bay.

Top middle: Organizational floor plan diagrams showing central core and circulation.

Top right: The terraced plan allows for planted green roofs above the first- and second-floor offices that reduce energy loads and manage stormwater runoff while enhancing the views. One of the ways storm water is retained on-site is by the use of more than three-quarters of an acre of green roofs. The green roofs are planted with succulents and other drought-tolerant species. Small terraces are carved out of each green roof and offer spectacular views across Sinclair Inlet to the Naval Shipyard in Bremerton.

Bottom left: View of Sinclair Inlet over vegetative roofs.

Bottom middle: Building model shown from the northwest.

Bottom right: Sectional study model.

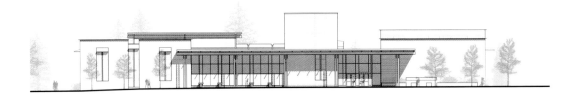

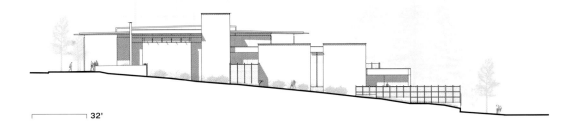

32'

Above, from top: South, West elevation
showing the Cline Street stairs,
East elevation.

Above: Rainwater falling on the building roofs is carried to the cisterns, which hold that water for irrigation use in dry months. The cisterns can hold more than 110,000 gallons of rainwater. After the site plants are established, the cisterns will be able to provide 100 percent of the annual irrigation needs on the site.

During the winter months, when the irrigation system is shut down, the cisterns will fill up and likely overflow. As this water spills out of the cistern structures, it is routed into a seasonal stream feature that parallels the Cline Avenue stairs. The water will wind its way down the hillside, culminating in a raingarden at the base of the slope, where it flows into the stormwater system.

Along the west side of the building, a grand staircase provides a comfortable means of ascending Cline Avenue. This staircase, which rises more that fifty vertical feet between Dwight Street and Division Street, will encourage the connection between the campus and downtown Port Orchard. In addition to providing a safe, direct pedestrian connection, the staircase will also host numerous overlooks and places to sit. It is seamlessly integrated into the landscape and coordinated with the new building in its overall configuration and material choices.

Top left: The main entry of the Kitsap County Administration Building is located on axis with the entrance to the Courthouse. The arrival sequence and experience was an important transition from the historic Courthouse. The new building entrance is amplified with a canopy and a clear view through the lobby to the stair below and the Naval Shipyard beyond.

Top right: In addition to offering aesthetic benefits to the employees, the green roofs primarily serve to provide a higher level of insulation value to the building. The green roof assemblies incorporate four inches of rigid isulation and six inches of topsoil. This thick blanket of materials helps keep the building cool in the summer and warm in the winter.

Opposite: Detail at south entry canopy showing narrow "vitrine" to display a glass canoe sculpture by artist Steven Maslach. The window allows for a view through the canoe to the commissioners' chambers.

Above: The deep 1½-story canopy over the main entrance provides shade for the south-facing glazed entry.

Opposite top: The Public counter is completely exposed to the street so as to provide a window on "your government at work."

Opposite bottom: The Public Counter serves the County Auditor Department. Folded cherry veneer acoustic wood panels unify the space and, due to the transparency of the facade, become a part of both the interior and exterior expression of the building.

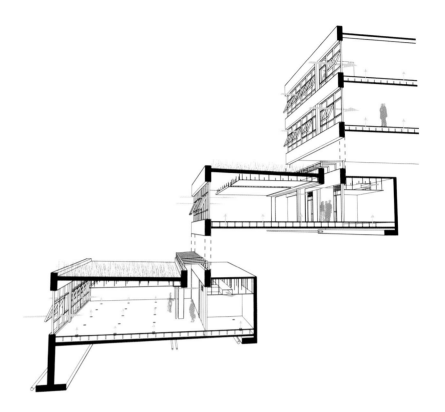

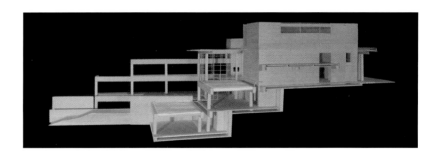

Opposite, top left: Main stair. The sky-lights correspond to the circulation elements and become a wayfinding device as you move through the building.

Opposite, top right: Office wing skylight occurs at the deepest point in the office floor.

Opposite, bottom: Detail at main stair using standard channel steel shapes and off-the-shelf bar grate as handrail.

Top: As with the Pierce County Environmental Services Building, the design team integrated building systems to achieve maximum performance. In this case the terraced building form allowed for operable windows at every level, which provided fresh air intake for the office areas. Heated and cooled air is fed from the raised-floor system and collected air is returned high along the enclosed offices at the linear skylights.

Bottom: Section model studying the day-light penetration into each office level.

Opposite: The main circulation spine receives natural light for three levels from the skylights above and has views to Sinclair Inlet beyond.

Following spread: A series of oil paintings on canvas were provided by Frank Samuelson depicting the salmon's migration. They conceal the acoustic treatment above.

Top left and right: Miller|Hull collaborated with three local artists to develop public art pieces that were integrated into the building design (rather than being placed at the completion of construction). David Franklin provided a series of large sliding doors to secure department offices at night but leave the main lobby open for meetings and events. The doors are either hand-carved and painted wood or water jet–cut steel plate. Basalt stone sculptures were provided by Will Robinson.

Bottom left: The overflow space from the council chambers has become an informal gathering spot for meetings and events.

FISHER PAVILION AT THE SEATTLE CENTER / Seattle, Washington

Overview

Fisher Pavilion is a 24,000-square-foot flexible exhibition space, located in the heart of the Seattle Center. This new building replaced the original "Flag Pavilion" that was built as a temporary structure in 1962 for the World's Fair. The new facility needed to house a wide range of year-round events, as well as augment cultural festivals on the public green that bring more than nine hundred thousand people to the Seattle Center each year.

Design Vision

After more than thirty years of use, the "temporary" Flag Pavilion structure needed to be replaced. The board at the Seattle Center asked Miller|Hull to design a new, more functional building on the existing site. By exploiting a grade change at the site, it was possible to insert the building into the land. This allowed for the creation of a civic plaza rooftop that is accessible from natural grade at the Children's Theatre above, while the exhibition space is partially excavated into the site, connecting it to the grade below, tying it directly into the International Fountain. This gesture restored the original master plan principles of the Seattle Center while updating the flexible exhibition space that the Seattle Center has found invaluable over the years.

Execution

The earth-sheltered concept takes advantage of the earth temperature of fifty-five degrees to wrap the building in a blanket of benign temperature, greatly reducing winter heating and summer cooling loads. Even though latent heat is generated by large crowds, it can be balanced by passive cooling and destratification fans. The entire north facade of Fisher Pavilion is clad in twenty-foot-high glazed roll-up sectional garage doors, offering views and direct connections to the central green. These vertical-lift automatic doors provide a kinetic quality to the space, opening or closing depending on the venue and the season. The doors also provide convenient access for vehicles during the set-up and take-down stage of Seattle Center events. The structure consists of long-span (seventy feet) prestressed concrete bulb t-beams supported on cast-in-place concrete columns and precast girders. Two vertical concrete pylons signal entry points, house elevators, and conceal mechanical equipment. A two-story service corridor and mechanical mezzanine allows reconfiguration of the exhibition space by staff, even during events. The corridor provides access to mechanical, electrical, and lighting systems as well as to AV equipment, catering kitchens, and the chillers used for the temporary ice-skating rink set up every holiday season.

Opposite: North facade of the pavilion.

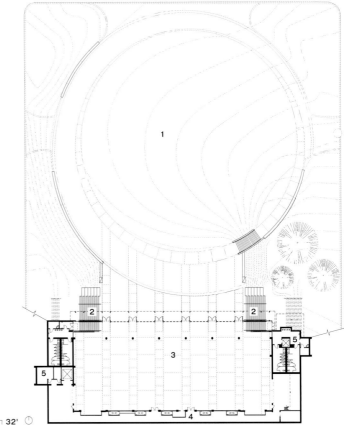

Above: The building becomes a backdrop
to the public green. The Children's Theater
is the barrel-vaulted red brick structure
just beyond the upper plaza.

Right: Main-level floor plan of the site.
Key: (1) Central green, (2) Indoor/outdoor
stairs and seat walls, (3) exhibition hall,
(4) service corridor, (5) service pylon.

32'

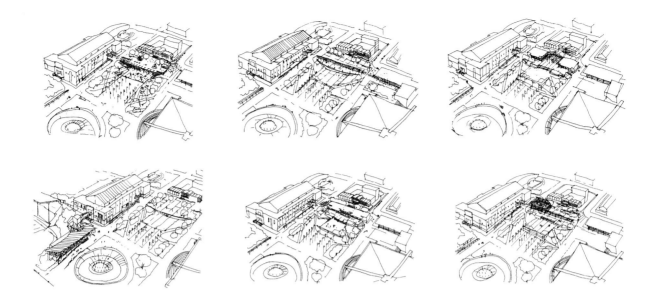

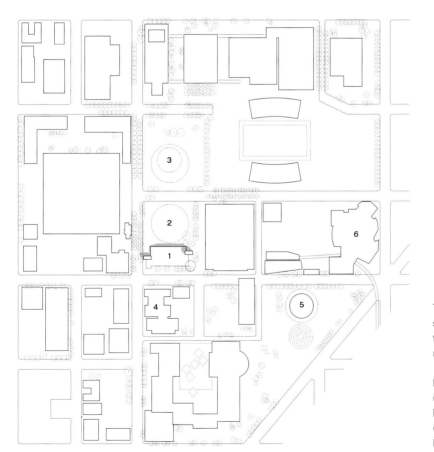

Top series: Early sketches of the site, shown here, were drawn in sequence to explore above- and below-grade massing options.

Left: Vicinity plan. Key: (1) Fisher Pavilion, (2) Central Green, (3) International Fountain, (4) Children's Museum, (5) Space Needle, (6) Experience Music Project.

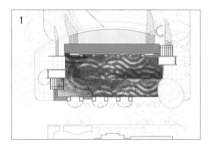

Top series of four: Construction shots showing installation of precast concrete bulb t-beams. The bridge technology of the precast bulb t-beams allowed for a high live load, long span, relatively shallow structure, and much faster installation than other more conventional systems.

Bottom series of four: The design of the plaza paving was an important consideration for the design team, as it can be seen from the Space Needle. (The team often refers to the plaza as the "fifth elevation" of the building.) There is a reoccuring device at Seattle Center of circles inscribed in squares that began as part of the 1962 World's Fair, as seen in the Space Needle and the International Fountain. This history led to the abstracted raindrops design for the plaza deck. (1) A computer rendering shows the "pixilated" paver design study of the rooftop plaza, (2) Photograph of raindrops translated into individual pavers. (3) the final paver pattern consisting of seven colors in 12 x 12 in. tiles abstracts the original raindrops pattern, (4) aerial view showing the rooftop, green, and international fountain.

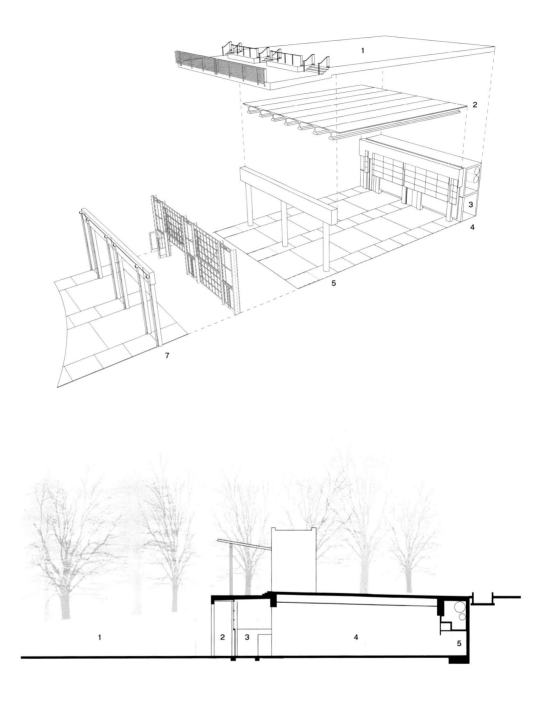

Top: Exploded axonometric showing typical structural bay. All the vertical structural elements are cast-in-place concrete, and all the horizontal elements are precast concrete.

Key, top: (1) Roof deck and Pavers, (2) precast bulb t-beams, (3) utility mezzanine, (4) service corridor, (5) primary structure, (6) envelope, (7) secondary structure.

Key, bottom (cross section): (1) green, (2) porch, (3) foyer, (4) exhibit, (5) service corridor.

Top: A cast-in-place concrete stair stretches from inside the building to outside, transitioning into a stepped seat wall and ultimately the landscape beyond.

Bottom left: View through open vertical lift door to International Fountain.

Bottom right: Study model of west side of building.

Opposite: Detail showing the layers of structure that define the transition zone between inside and out. The site stairs begin as seat/retaining walls and continue inside. The outboard narrow double columns demark the porch zone. The operable envelope blurs the line between the porch and the interior foyer. The main structural columns inside are the boundary at which the interior space can be completely blacked out for certain events.

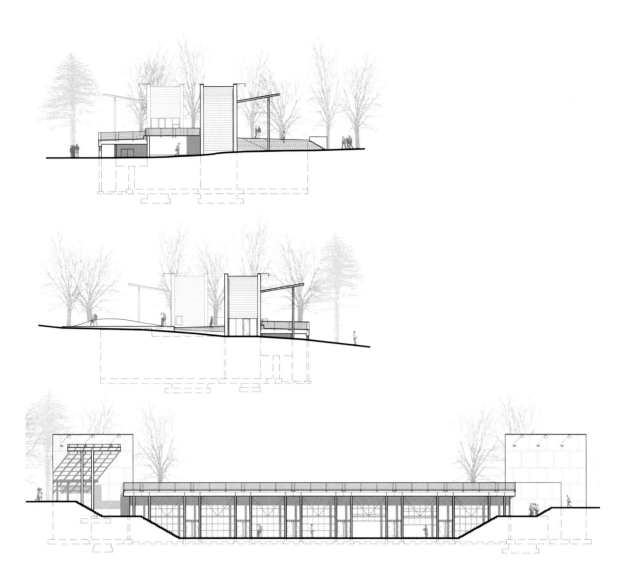

Above, from top: West, East, and
North elevations.

Opposite: The concrete "pylons" that
house the elevators and core are conceived
as pairs of plates, as is the tilted glass
canopy that drains through a slot in the
concrete wall of the east pylon.

Following spread: Composite photograph
showing the organization of the ceiling.
The floor had to be kept free from
any devises due to its multiuse nature.

All power and service had to come
from drops in the ceiling. The ceiling is
composed of concrete structural bulb
t-beams, mechanical ducting, destratification fans and electrical cable trays.
A pipe grid suspended in the bays of the
structure allows the lighting, speakers,
power, and decorations to be configured
depending on the current event.

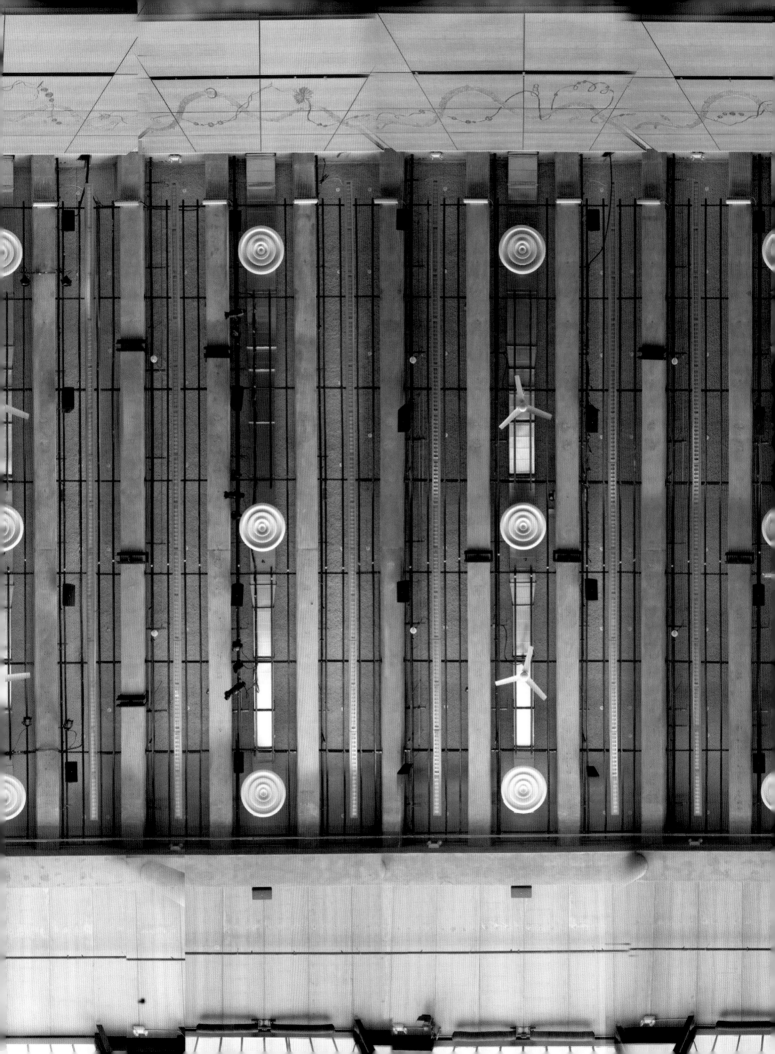

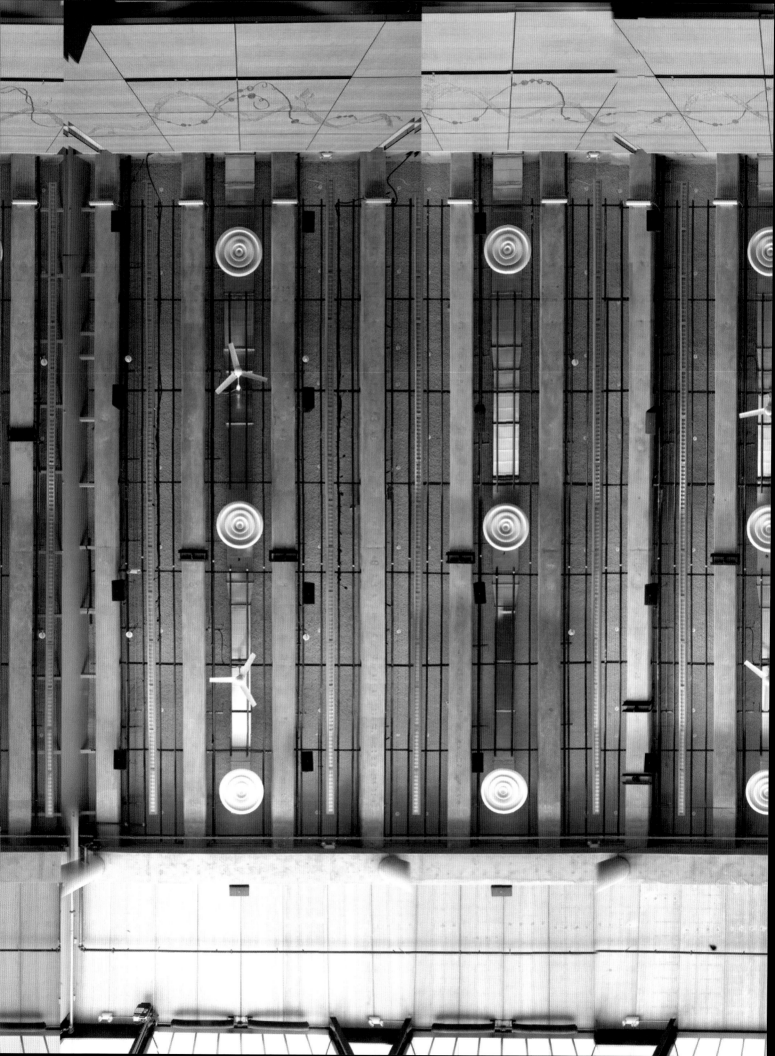

Above: (1) Fisher Pavilion is the hub for many Seattle summer festivals, (2) group gathering on the upper plaza steps, (3) The glazing enclosure is separate from the structure, (4) The Eyes Wide Open exhibit of empty boots honoring each U.S. military casualty from the war in Iraq, (5) The exhibition space is set up for a nationally televised Professional Bowling Association event in January 2004, (6) The transparent facade helps to activate the green at night, (7) Miller|Hull's thirtieth anniversary party; the temperate climate allows the garage doors to remain open for events, encouraging people to equally use the outside and the inside, (8) An exterior row of columns creates a front porch, (9) The Space Needle and Fisher Pavilion lit for the holidays, (10) The flexible space can incorporate many kinds of multimedia displays.

Above: The open flexible space allows the Fisher Pavilion to host many special events and exhibitions.

Following spread: During the winter months, the interior is converted to an ice-skating rink.

OLYMPIC COLLEGE–POULSBO / Poulsbo, Washington

Overview

Located amid the dense growth of fir trees and bordering the rural yet rapidly growing urban center of Poulsbo, Washington, this self-contained Olympic College
campus serves the needs of an entire community college. Miller|Hull was selected
after completing the Shelton, Washington, branch campus for Olympic College.
The twenty-acre site was part of a two-hundred-acre parcel slated for private development. The design phase for this project took place from 1995 through 1997. The
project was then put on hold for several years while development regulations for
surrounding parcels of land were resolved. In 2004 construction was finally able to
commence, with occupancy in 2006.

Two influential factors led the design. First, the creation of a "campus in the
forest" became a defining influence on the architectural massing and the choice of
materials. This goal evolved out of a community-based design process. The desire
was to plan the site development in a way that would save a buffer of second- and
third-growth coniferous forest around the entire perimeter of the site, shielding it
from the adjacent commercial development. The second significant influence came
from the area's strong Nordic heritage. In fact, there was a land-use code requirement on the project to "include architectural features that reflect the Scandinavian
heritage of the settlement."

The building program includes classrooms, a science laboratory, writing and
computer labs, distance-learning classrooms, an auditorium, faculty offices, and
student-support areas, including a study lounge, a student commons area, and a
bookstore.

Olympic College–Shelton was an earlier
project for the same client.

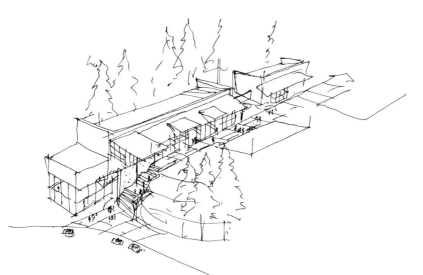

Top: Entry Plaza

Bottom: A close interface between the building and the wooded landscape is maintained via the primary entry plaza, pedestrian spine, and terraces.

Design Vision

When the Miller|Hull team first walked the site, it was only accessible by a logging road. The understory was so thick below the third-growth stand of Douglas fir trees that it was difficult to see more than fifty feet in the distance. On these early visits, the team discovered a few site features to which they could respond. First, running diagonally across the site was a twenty-foot-high rift that formed an upper bench to the east. The other site features of significance were closed depressions that later were converted to stormwater detention basins. The rift allowed the lower floor to open to the main parking lot below and placed the majority of the new building at the upper campus elevation, with views beyond the parking area below to the retained forest buffer. The roof deck built over a portion of the lower level creates a south-facing plaza, spilling out of the upper level of the building and providing a gathering spot for students year-round.

Execution

The floor plan organizes the academic spaces within a simple brick-faced bar, allowing north-facing natural light into the classrooms. South of the main corridor are the more open public spaces, such as the student lounge and study space. This floor plan diagram is clearly expressed in the building form. The brick bar runs continuously through the building and is visible from the interior and exterior. The more public spaces are registered against the brick wall and open up to the landscape through more extensive glazing.

The building responds to the climate of the Pacific Northwest through the use of large glazed walls that extend to the natural environment. Exterior materials wrap inside the building, expressing the building organization and strengthening the indoor-outdoor relationship. The dramatic forms evoke images of the Scandinavian heritage yet make a larger civic statement for the college. However historic, these influences remain true to a modern expression and blend well with exposed steel structure and cast-in-place concrete. The extensive use of wood—exposed wood beams, fir decking, and cedar cladding—recall typical Scandinavian materiality, while connecting the building to its place in the forested Pacific Northwest.

Opposite top: Site plan. Key:
(1) Forest, (2) wetland, (3) lower parking,
(4) Entry Plaza / Hillclimb, (5) upper
parking, (6) Olympic College-Poulsbo
main building, (7) service building.

Opposite left, below: The massive brick
wall emphasizes the programmatic break
between the social and academic spaces.

Opposite right, below: The vehicular
access was planned carefully to retain
the mature trees and natural landscape
in the building's foreground.

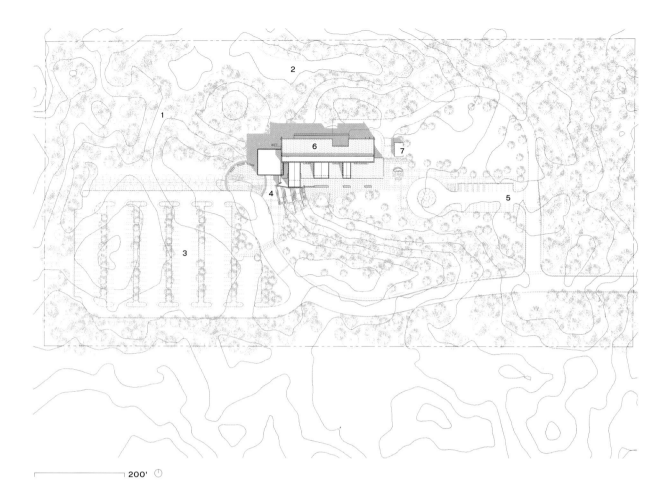

200' ⊘

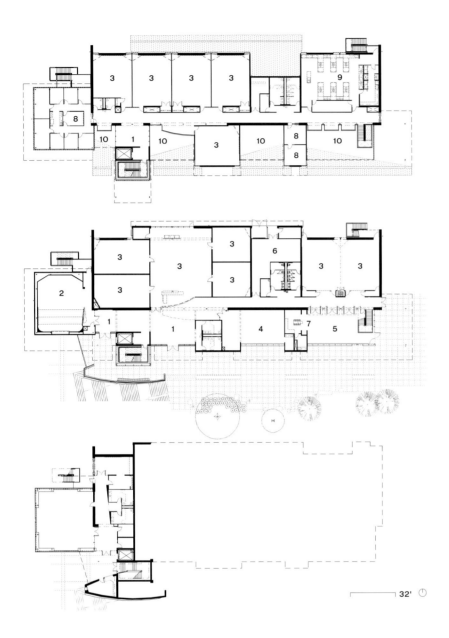

From top: Second-floor plan, first-floor
plan, lower level floor-plan. Key: (1) Entry
and lobby, (2) auditorium, (3) classrooms
and computer labs, (4) student lounge,
(5) student commons, (6) receiving,
(7) food service, (8) offices and
conference rooms, (9) science laboratory,
(10) open to below.

Right: Plan diagram showing the main
program elements, administrative,
academic, and social.

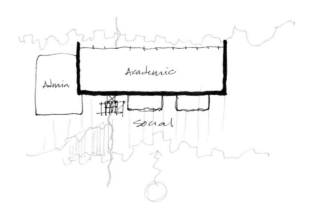

Above: The building straddles the natural twenty-foot rift in the site. The interior and exterior vertical circulation is strategically located along this rift.

Above: Center-hung rotating partitions provide flexibility in the student commons area, which allows for collegewide gatherings by connecting to the classroom space across the hall. The stair connects the two academic levels directly to the commons.

Above: The view from the commons area opens out to the preserved landscape buffer. Through the design of highly flexible classrooms in a variety of sizes, the college is able to offer many diverse programs to the community. Courses range from computer training to wine tasting; the building accommodates all with ease. Local community events can also be accommodated in the facility, providing a venue for after-hours events.

Left: A two-story commons area provides natural light and open gathering space. The rotating partitions are shown closed here.

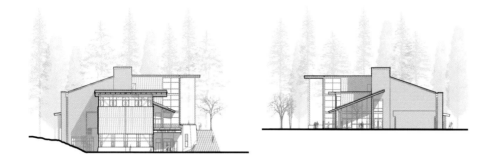

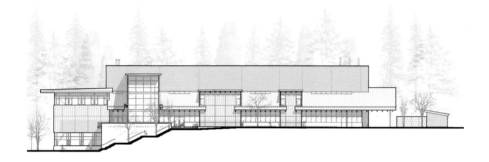

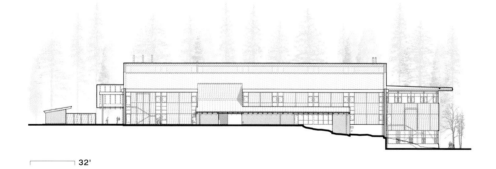

32'

Clockwise from top left: West, East, South,
and North elevations

Top left: Significant emphasis is placed on the transparent main stair in an effort to encourage the use of the stair over the elevators.

Bottom left: The glazed stair provides a panoramic territorial view which includes Mount Rainier.

Above right: The main stair tower has an exposed steel structure and expansive glass walls, as seen from the main entrance plaza flanked by Native American sculpture commissioned by OCP under Washington State Arts Commission Art in Public Places program.

Opposite: Detail showing the Scandinavian-influenced materials palette consisting of clear-finish cedar siding, steel, and cast concrete.

Top: The second-floor hallway opens to the commons below and provides pockets for informal study.

Bottom: Careful thought was given to the integration of details at the moments where people interact with the building. At the entrance to the lecture hall, the handrail wraps around the wall and also integrates a shallow counter for laying out books and handouts for class.

Following spread: The natural landscape is retained to provide a forested setting for the campus.

UNIVERSITY OF WASHINGTON CONIBEAR SHELLHOUSE
AND ATHLETIC CENTER / Seattle, Washington

Overview

The University of Washington's Conibear Shellhouse and Athletic Center houses three main functions: the university's rowing program, a 250-seat dining facility for the athletic programs, and Student Academic Services. The new building reuses foundations from the old shellhouse to preserve the location at the water's edge—something that would not be possible with current shoreline restrictions. While the original structure was built on the site of a former city dump that was one of the largest peat bogs in the state, today the site is some of the most picturesque waterfront property on Lake Washington. The shellhouse's location—with newly restored wetlands and pathways that link to existing nature walks and public access to the shoreline—makes it ideal as a student center. In addition, its location near campus ballfields and the football stadium allows the building to be a convenient stop for all student athletes, uniting their services under one roof. The site is dramatic for viewing crew races and hosting special university events, but also provides an inspiring daily backdrop for the rigorous routine of the student athlete.

Design Vision

Although the site had been the home of the University of Washington's acclaimed rowing program since 1949, there was a desire to create a center that brought all student athletes together and reflected all the programs of the university's Athletic Department. The challenge of this dual-identity was solved by creating two distinct entrances: one from the west, at the main level, which serves the entire campus, and a second, lower-level entry from the south, at water level, which was historically (and remains today) exclusively the crew's entrance.

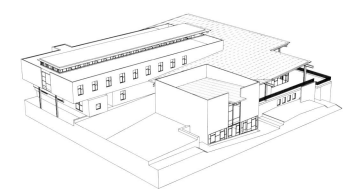

Top: The size and process for deploying the oars and shells from the storage level was a defining design consideration for the crew bays that open directly out to the water.

Bottom: Study axonometric drawing showing the main forms of the building.

Execution

The new building was built up from the existing pile foundation that encroaches on current shoreline setback requirements at the eastern edge of the site. The university's rowing program occupies the lower level; the shell storage bays rest along the water's edge. Large operable glass sectional doors display the shells and also provide direct access to the docks for launching. Beyond the shell storage, cutting deeper into the existing slope, are large training workout spaces for athlete conditioning and crew team meetings. Behind these are the locker facilities.

Several factors led to a naturally ventilated building solution, including the prevailing wind direction and the fact that the building is partially earth sheltered. The openings required are at water level. This naturally occurring stack effect is enhanced by a series of motorized louvers that pull cool air through ventilation shafts from Lake Washington through the concrete mass of the shell storage bays into the team workout areas.

The dining area for all of the athletic programs occupies much of the main level and has views to the water beyond an outdoor terrace. The terrace provides prime viewing of the world-class regattas the university hosts. The dining function is mostly transparent, expressed as a large, sloped steel and timber roof form that sits on the concrete structure below. A glass floor and open stair at the entry lobby and student lounge visually connect the dining function to the shell bay area below. A lecture hall anchors the entry along with an accessible on-grade green roof that is located over the locker rooms. The upper level consists of Student Academic Services, expressed as metal-clad forms inserted into the sloped roof. Academic functions here include computer training, access to advisers, and private and group study areas.

Right: Interior and exterior views of the existing coach's boathouse, designed by Miller|Hull in 1993. Situated directly adjacent to the Conibear shellhouse, it provides a smaller scaled complement to the new building.

Opposite: The building was designed to use the foundations of the original structure, which allowed it to be completely situated in a protected wetland surrounded by habitat trails.

Above: (1–2) The new Conibear shellhouse was built on the foundations of the original seen in its location on the same site in 1949. The design for the new shellhouse gained inspiration not only from the waterfront site, which allows a direct connection to the water for the crew; but more importantly from the long-standing legacy of the University of Washington rowing teams. (3–4) Shellhouse today and in the 1950s. (5–6) Balcony, today and in the 1950s, still provides the best view of the boat launch. (7) World-renowned shell builder George Pocock discussing a design with Husky coaches. (8–9) Historic shots of the Husky crew in the 1950s. (10–11) The "Mountlake Cut" has been used by the crew since 1903 and provides just one of the many sheltered waterways that allows them to practice year round. (12) Being close to the water is an affinity not only for the University crew teams, but for Miller|Hull, seen above on the shores of the Agate Passage embarking on the annual firm kayak trip that takes place each summer.

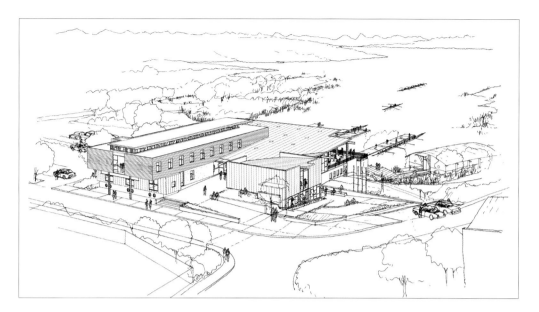

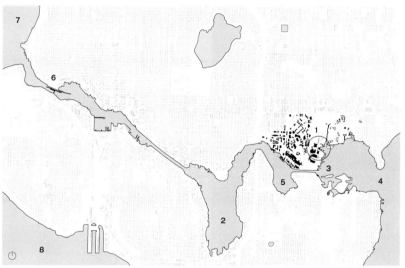

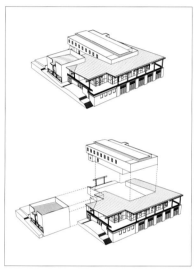

Top: Design study aerial drawing including its waterfront site. At lower right of the image is the coach's boathouse.

Bottom right: Axonometric drawings of the building taken from the waterfront side of the project illustrating the building's clear formal expression as a function of programmatic organization within the building. The athletic dining room faces the water, while the education and administration and study halls face the street—shown extracted from the sloped dining room form. The large tutoring space is also shown extracted. The roof form was designed as a compositional element or "tray" that intersects and organizes the main program elements.

Above left: Vicinity map of (1) the University of Washington campus with its proximity to (2) Lake Union, (3) the Montlake Cut, (4) Lake Washington, (5) Portage Bay, (6) Ballard Locks, (7) Puget Sound, and (8) Elliot Bay. The University of Washington is the only campus in the U.S. that lies directly on waterfront property. This vicinity provides seven different routes that allow the rowers to practice year-round and in different weather conditioins. The waterway is also shared by leisure boat traffic and connects the fresh water of Lake Washington to the salt water of Puget Sound.

Following spread: The new shellhouse seen from the water, illuminating the shoreline during early morning workouts. The coach's boathouse is seen at left.

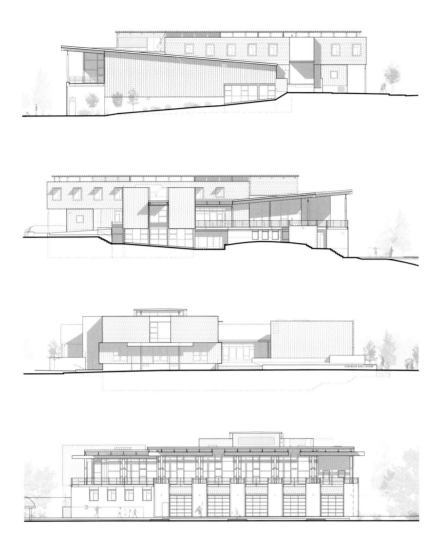

Above from top: North elevation, South elevation, West elevation, and East elevation.

Right: A structural axonometric drawing and physical study model were tools used to develop the structural expression seen at the water side of the shellhouse. Since the team was reusing the existing concrete pilings, column load locations were predetermined. Steel frames were designed to branch out to carry sections of the roof load, and transfer it down to the existing piling locations. Visually, they create overscaled frames or "windows" for viewers to watch crew events from the upper deck.

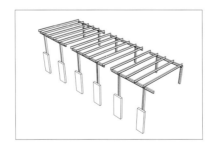

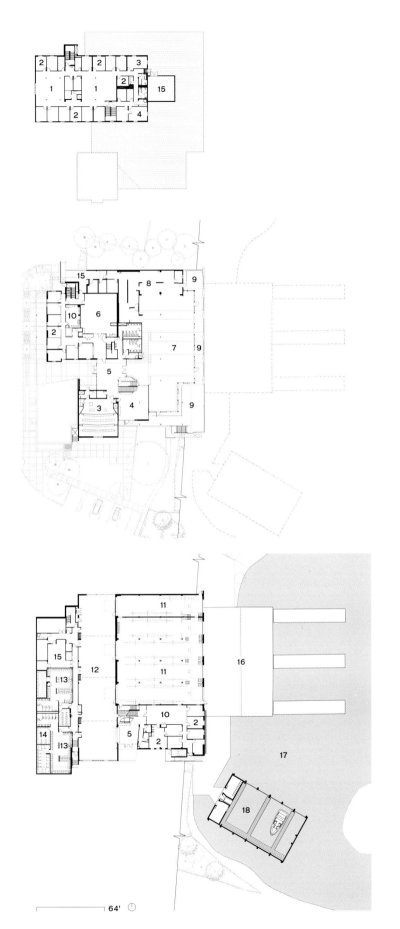

64'

Left, from top: Upper floor, main floor, and lower crew level. Key: (1) Study hall, (2) office, (3) tutoring space, (4) lounge, (5) lobby, (6) computer lab, (7) dining hall, (8) kitchen, (9) deck, (10) meeting room, (11) shell bays, (12) team training room, (13) locker rooms, (14) drying rooms, (15) mechanical/electrical/storage, (16) dock, (17) Union Bay on Lake Washington, (18) coach's boathouse.

Opposite top: The interior of the athlete's dining room overlooking the water. The Husky Clipper, a George Pocock–designed shell, adorns the ceiling in the main dining space. The U.S. crew won the Gold Medal in this shell at the 1936 Olympic Games in Berlin.

Opposite bottom: Training rooms on the lower level allow the team to hold workouts in the same building as their study and tutoring facilities. In order for the room to get natural light, the space was stretched across the full length of the building and grade was adjusted at the ends to allow for large windows. To take advantage of the cool shell bays and prevailing wind off the lake, glazed garage doors open directing into the shell storage, which allows low velocity air to naturally ventilate the space.

Above left: The visual connection that joins the street level entry lobby to the lower crew level is the main stair enclosed in glass. The partial glass floor at the stair opening allows views directly into the shell storage bays.

Above right: View down the stairway from the street level entry lobby.

Above top: Study rendering showing the potential view from the athlete's dining hall. This view allows for audiences to watch crew matches from above and indoors. It also creates a dramatic backdrop for a special event space available for athletic department programs.

Opposite: The detail photograph shows how the main structure is separated from the glazed envelope. This layering reinforces the inside/outside transition. Continuing the glass up in between the structural members allows the plane of the roof deck to read as uninterrupted.

Above from left to right: The glazed entry "gasket" separates the administration/ study hall from the tutoring space box. The building is seen from the south with canted roof opening out the water view. Again, the entry "gasket" is seen shaping the approach plaza from the street. Lastly, the large overhang creates a viewing porch for crew events or spill-out space for day-to-day dining. The exposed steel frames give definition and prominence to the porch when seen from the water.

Following spread: Crew members have a large prep, warm-up, and cleaning space right at water's edge. The wood boardwalk is flush with the original concrete platform slab, which becomes the floor level of the interior shell bays, seen beyond. A new lightweight building had to be designed to meet the loads of the existing foundation. The lightness is articulated by "floating" the roof above the glass box.

ADDITION TO THE ART AND ARCHITECTURE BUILDING,

UNIVERSITY OF MICHIGAN / Ann Arbor, Michigan

Overview

This "on the boards" addition to the University of Michigan's Art + Architecture Building adds studio space, crit space, and offices, as well as research space, class-rooms, and a reading room. The third floor of the original 1973 building houses crit spaces for all student levels directly adjacent to the studios, which are noisy, active, crowded areas that give a unique feel to the school. Professors' offices, located near the studios, are easily accessible by students. Housed in high-bay shop areas on the ground floor is a highly respected building technology program, where research continues in energy conservation, lighting design, and construction.

All of these spaces needed more capacity, and the college wanted to preserve the adjacencies that give the school its dynamic, creative atmosphere. In addition, the school was interested in promoting the strong culture of the architecture pro-gram. There was a desire for the building to "be seen" and to be understandable as the home of the architecture and planning departments.

Design Vision

The site selected for this addition is the roof area over existing high-bay shops on the south side of the building, which is ideal for linking directly into the existing studios, crit spaces, and offices. The south-facing facade was designed to be trans-parent, open to campus visibility and views, and readily tapped for energy and sustainable strategies. The Miller|Hull team explored several expressions of this concept to respond to the harsh Michigan climate and minimize energy use.

The south facade was initially conceived as a double skin, with crit boxes perched along the length of the research bay below. The crit spaces would be expressed as individual rooms adjacent to the studios, while students could occupy the space between the skin system as an informal work or gathering space: the idea of "living within the skin" would place students and their work on display for the campus.

Execution

Further design evolution led to the notion of the crit space as an open gallery instead of a dedicated "room." This would preserve the relationship between studio and crit space but create a more flexible space that could be combined or separated as required. The team also explored the skin as a single layer augmented with shading devices, in lieu of an occupiable zone. Movable portions of the shades could optimize or minimize solar gain. Sliding doors would connect the crit gal-lery to the outdoors, while providing projection surfaces both inside and outside the building.

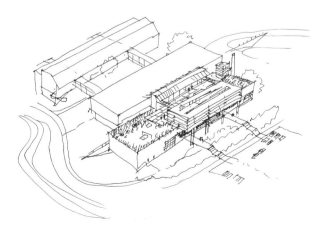

Above: An early scheme distinguished by its double skin had operable sections that opened the studio to the outdoors.

Left: This conceptual sketch from the first interview describes perched forms capitalizing on the unique rooftop site. The location above the existing research bays provides a new "front door" to the school while connecting the college's three departments.

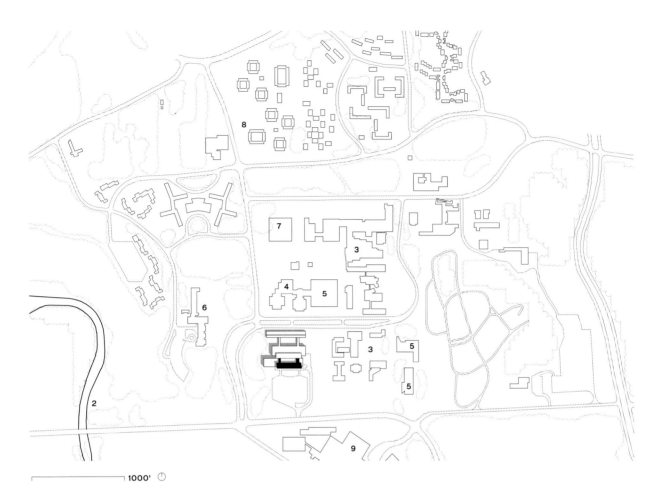

1000' ⊙

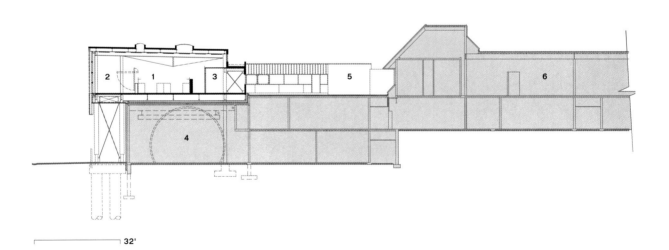

32'

Top: University of Michigan North Campus Map. Key: (1) Art + Architecture Building, (2) Huron River, (3) engineering buildings, (4) commons, (5) library, (6) School of Music, (7) Drama Center, (8) student housing, (9) VA Hospital.

Bottom: A building section shows the integration of the existing building and the addition. New offices, studios, and critique spaces live above the existing high-bay research spaces. Key: (1) Studio, (2) gallery space, (3) faculty office, (4) existing research lab, (5) light court, (6) existing studio.

Above: The perched crit boxes and spaces within the double skin provide cover for exterior materials testing yard. Sections of the skin fold up or flip out to control temperature, air flow, and connection to the outdoors.

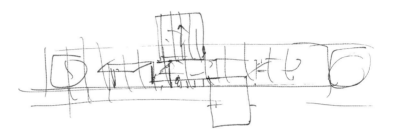

Opposite: Early sketches show the design evolution of the spatial qualities and the exterior expression of the crit boxes and their relationship to the studio space. The design team also studied the nature of the covered exterior space created by the new addition. The space operates both as a working materials research yard and as a generous entry to the existing building.

Top: A progress rendering shows the initial double-skin concept, with the building name visible on the glass to create campus visibility and identity.

Bottom: This early conceptual sketch of the south facade reveals enclosure elements that could slide up or down.

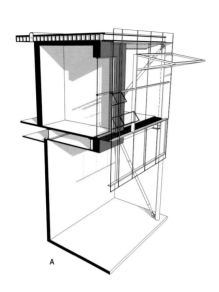

A

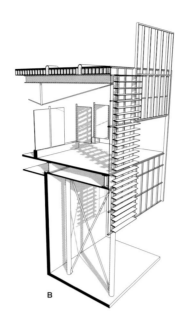

B

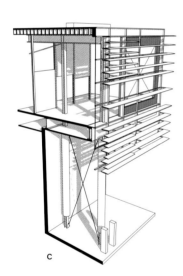

C

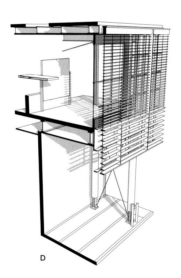

D

A series of section perspective diagrams show a portion of the building at the south elevation and speak to the design evolution of the facade and crit walls.

Scheme (A) shows the original crit box and occupiable double-skin concept. Shading was accomplished by the roof of the double-skin zone, which allowed an facade to be uninterrupted transparent glass.

Scheme (B) shows early transformation to a crit gallery and the first use of a single-skin system with vertical sliding doors. Fixed louvers shade the glazing. A continuation of the crit gallery concept, scheme (C) shows fixed louvers of varying depth and spacing in an attempt to provide rhythm and to illustrate shading design concepts to students within. The scheme also shows the appearance of colorful

sliding doors with translucent glazing. The doors were designed to provide digital projection surfaces both inside and outside the buiding. In Scheme (D) operable exterior blinds are included to optimize solar gain. These are supported within a steel armature, which could also be used for testing building system technology and highlighting architectural research already taking place within the college.

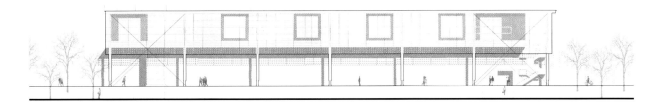

32'

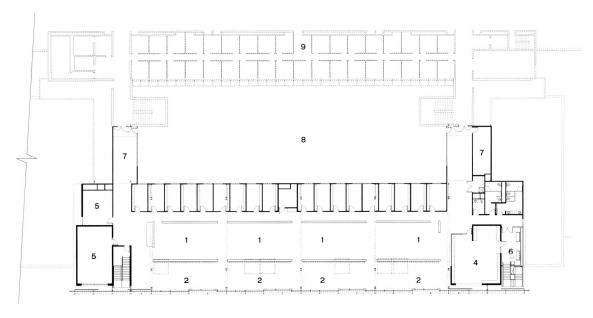

32'

Top: A progress drawing of the South elevation showing shading devices.

Bottom: Further design iteration led to a crit gallery instead of separate crit boxes. Key: (1) Studio, (2) crit gallery, (3) faculty offices, (4) reading room, (5) classrooms, (6) deck, (7) social nook, (8) light court, (9) existing offices.

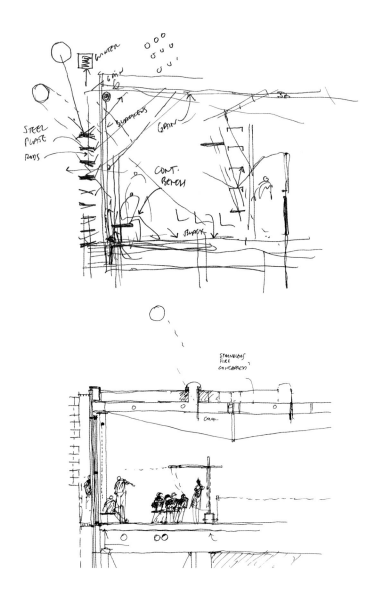

Above: Progress sketches used to explore daylight and shading strategies and the sectional qualities of the crit and studio spaces.

Opposite top: Through a series of enlarged study models, the team explored methods of detailing the ceiling that evolved into a three-layered system: acoustic attenuation, daylighting via skylights, and electric light fixtures. This allowed a repetitive and functional yet expressive ceiling. These models were used for daylighting studies of the addition and helped the team optimize solar control and daylighting.

Opposite bottom: A model showing one bay of the addition, including the layered facade, layered ceiling, and exterior workyard.

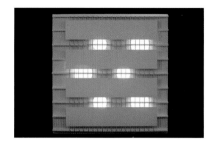  

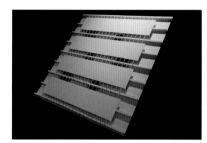 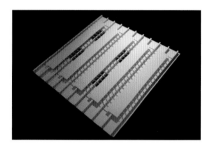 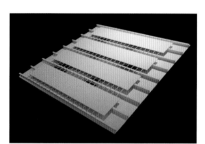

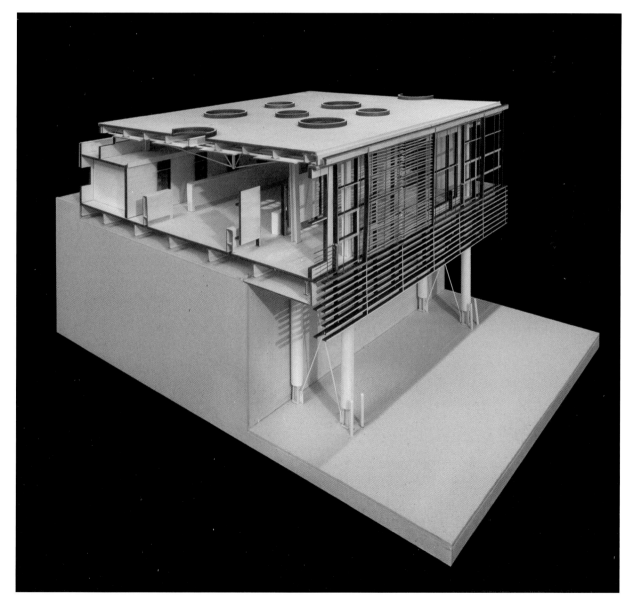

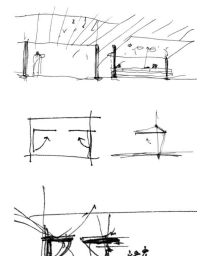

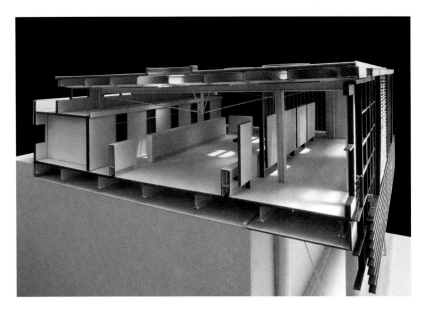

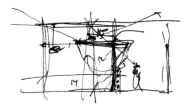

Top and bottom, left: Photographs of a larger physical model showing open studio and crit gallery with crit partitions and layered ceiling.

Above right: Progress sketches were used to study the possibilities of the operable crit walls separating the studios from the crit gallery space. The design team focused on ease of operation, scale, dual purpose operation, and daylighting in evaluating the various tectonic options.

Opposite top: A progress rendering of the building showing operable shading devices and sliding curtainwall doors.

Opposite bottom: Process sketch showing the effects of the louver elements on daylight entering the space as well as the creation of shade for the exterior on-grade research yard.

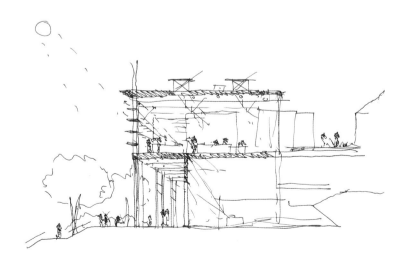

1310 E. UNION LOFTS / Seattle, Washington

Overview

Located at the edge of the Pike Street and Pine Street corridor in downtown Seattle, this public transit–oriented neighborhood is populated by mixed-use developments. The forty-by-eighty-foot site comprised an infill (midblock) plot, smaller than a typical single-family residential lot in Seattle. This reality made program fulfillment and construction a unique challenge. However, both the client and design team felt strongly about creating a livable, well-located example of urban housing in an already walkable transit-linked area—setting the precedent for urban housing as a contributing force behind a successful neighborhood.

Design Vision

Seattle's multifamily urban housing is almost entirely designed with one-story bases of concrete, enclosing retail and parking, and upper-story wood-frame residential units expressed as boxes with "punched" smaller-scale windows. While this was a viable way to organize the program, it also rendered the residential aspect of the building somewhat invisible. As a reinvention of this urban housing model, the Miller|Hull team envisioned a simpler unified form that came down and engaged the street with substantial glazing. This would allow the occupants' lifestyles to create the project's sense of style. To accomplish this, the building became an image of structural architecture, conveying a sense of economy, efficiency, discipline, and order.

Execution

Given the small site, with essentially no lay-down area, a steel structure provided the contractor with a rapid erection sequence. The primary gravity-load system is coated with fire-retardant, intumescent paint, and the diagonal bracing and mezzanine structure is exposed steel. Glass and aluminum-frame garage doors roll up, converting the living and dining spaces to exterior balconies. Floor plans of the loft-style units are completely open, with only the bathrooms enclosed. The units on the second through the fourth floors run front to back, wrapping around a compact core housing an elevator, stair, and shafts. The fifth-floor units have private roof terraces off the mezzanine level and a spiral stair to an additional roof deck. This layout allows upper units with a two-story loft layout to use west-facing balconies, to take advantage of dramatic city and mountain views.

Opposite: The lofts at 1310 E. Union, Miller|Hull's first urban housing project, created a more visible and unified residential example for downtown Seattle.

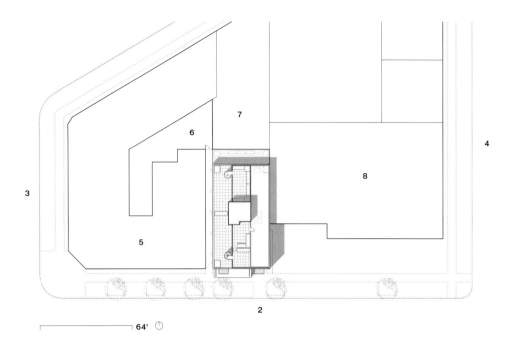

7

6

3

5

8

4

2

64'

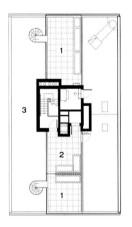
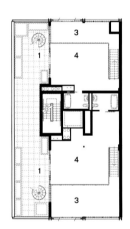

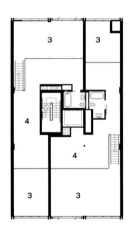

Bottom, floor plans from left: Roof terrace, 5th-floor mezzanine, 5th floor, 4th-floor mezzanine, 4th floor, 3rd floor, 2nd floor, ground-floor plan. The street-level plan provides retail space and access to the lower level parking. Key: (1) private deck, (2) public deck, (3) open to below, (4) upper loft to unit below, (5) main floor of unit, (6) shared vestibule, (7) private balcony, (8) garage entry, (9) private parking garage, (10) retail space.

Above, top: Site plan at 1310 E. Union showing the building's tight site and infill condition. Key: (1) 1310 E. Union, (2) East Union Street, (3) 13th Avenue, (4) 14th Avenue, (5) existing four-story concrete building, (6) residential courtyard, (7–8) existing one-story concrete building.

Opposite, top: Within the unified form of the building, each unit is unique in plan and section, as is evident in this unit stack diagram. The 5th mezzanine floor through the 2nd floor include two units per floor that interlock both in plan and in section.

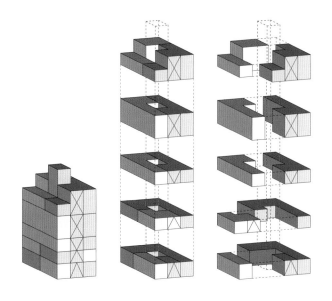

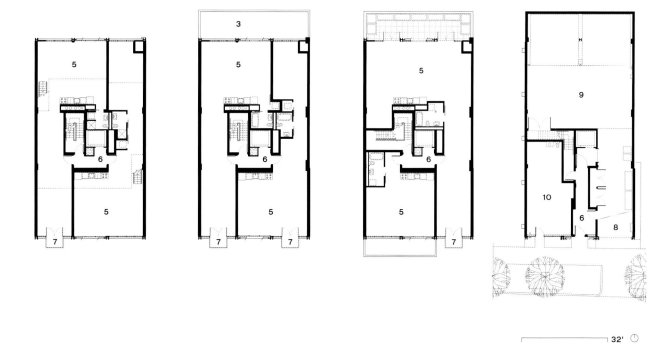

32'

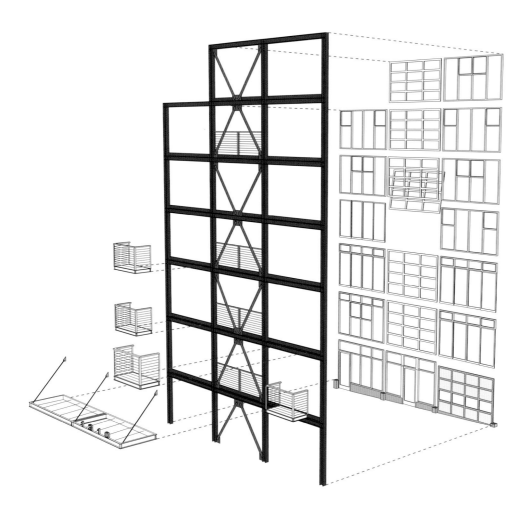

Above: The steel structure, shown in this exploded perspective diagram, became the iconic expression of the building.

Right: A detail of the building's balconies. The team's use of steel grating for the balcony surface eliminated the need for concealed waterproofing and lightens its structural appearance.

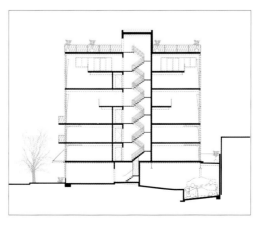

Above: South elevation

Far left: E. Union, with its rear elevation visible to the north from Pike Street.

Left: One of the innovations used on this project was a more efficient lift-style parking system. Two units share a lift, allowing double the amount of cars to be parked in a small space. The lift's size requires owners to own a compact car.

Above: View of surrounding Seattle from
the rooftop terrace. Seattle's temperate
climate allows for year-round use of this
outdoor living space.

Above: The upper mezzanine level of a
loft-style unit, with rooftop terrace visible
outside.

Above: Interior view of a loft-style
two-story unit.

Opposite: The glazed overhead door—
often used by Miller|Hull on small island
cabins—is an example of an off-the-shelf
product used in a unique manner to give
residents a large-scale two-story opening
facing the street.

156 W. SUPERIOR STREET / Chicago, Illinois

Overview

Located within the emerging River North district in downtown Chicago, the proposed condominium project at 156 W. Superior Street needed to blend with the existing brick and stone loft-type buildings in the area. It also needed to reflect the lifestyles of urban living expressed by the new housing, bars, restaurants, and galleries populating the neighborhood. The client had seen the firm's housing project in Seattle (1310 E. Union) and was interested in bringing a similar expression of modern urban living to Chicago. Like its predecessor, 1310, this building wanted to contribute to a "working" neighborhood, by providing housing within a dense urban fabric near public transit, workplace, and nightlife.

Design Vision

For this project the Miller|Hull team was inspired by Chicago's architectural tradition of creating elegant and well-detailed buildings. Active at the turn of the twentieth century, such architects as Louis Sullivan, Daniel Burnham, and William LeBaron Jenney were some of the first to utilize steel-frame construction in buildings. Adding to this unique Chicago context was the steel and glass language of what has been called the Second Chicago School, defined by the work of Ludwig Mies van der Rohe and early Skidmore, Owings & Merrill designs. A finely detailed steel structure contrasted with a glass enclosure was a distinguishing feature of this movement. With these strong traditions in mind, the 156 W. Superior building was envisioned as an exploration of the local craft and building customs, where structure should be the essence of the solution.

Execution

To articulate the building mass, a steel-frame structural bay fully enclosed in glass occupies the center portion of the south and north elevations. The lateral braced frame, which did not require fire-proofing over the steel, became the primary structural expression. By conveying these elevations as a series of two-story frames with steel X-braces, the building seems larger than its ninety-foot height and is able to hold its own in this area of tall buildings. The steel frames support cantilevered decks for each unit, enclosed with stainless-steel railings and louvers for privacy from adjacent development. A slablike element on the west side of the building, clad in standing-seam metal siding, forms a compositional counterpoint to the light structural frame. The building's base of concrete masonry provides a solid podium that visually supports the light steel and glass tower.

Opposite: 156 W. Superior at night, providing a visible example of housing in a dense urban neighborhood.

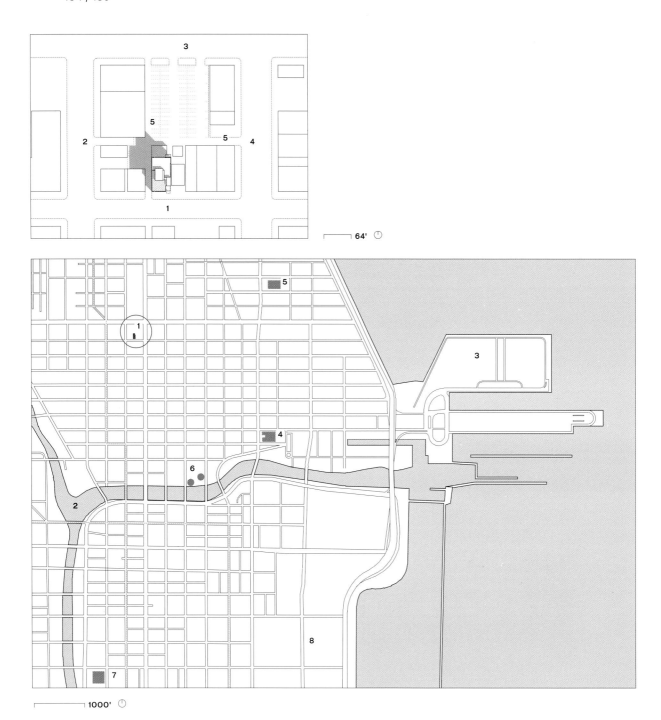

64'

1000'

Top: This vicinity plan places the 156 W. Superior building within its midblock infill site. Key: (1) West Superior Street, (2) North Wells Street, (3) West Chicago Avenue, (4) North La Salle Boulevard, (5) alley.

Bottom: This plan of downtown Chicago shows the river and the location of the growing River North neighborhood. Buildlings highlighted in grey reflect some of Chicago's iconic architectural landmarks. Key: (1) The 156 W. Superior site, (2) The Chicago River, (3) Navy Pier, (4) The Tribune Tower, (5) The Hancock Tower, (6) Marina City, (7) The Sears Tower, (8) Millennium Park.

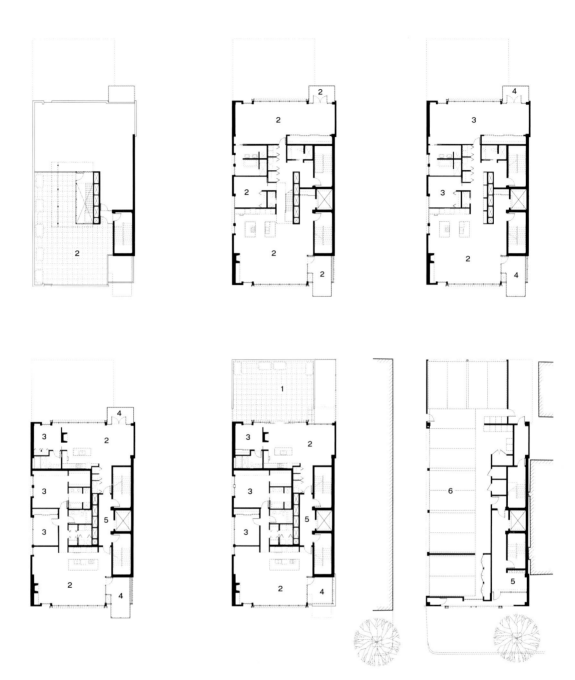

Top, left to right: Roof terrace plan, floor 9, and floors 5–8.

Bottom, left to right: Floors 3–4, floor 2, and ground floor.

Key: (1) Private terrace, (2) living/kitchen/dining room, (3) bedroom, (4) private balcony, (5) shared vestibule, (6) parking.

The roof and floor plans for levels 2–9 show the variety of units in the building as well as the outdoor space built into each unit. Floors 2 to 4 incorporate two smaller studio units, each accessible from a shared elevator lobby. However, floors 5 through 9 have only one unit each, receiving daylight from both north and south facades. The street-level plan shows covered parking stalls accessed from the alley as well as a shared interior elevator and stair lobby.

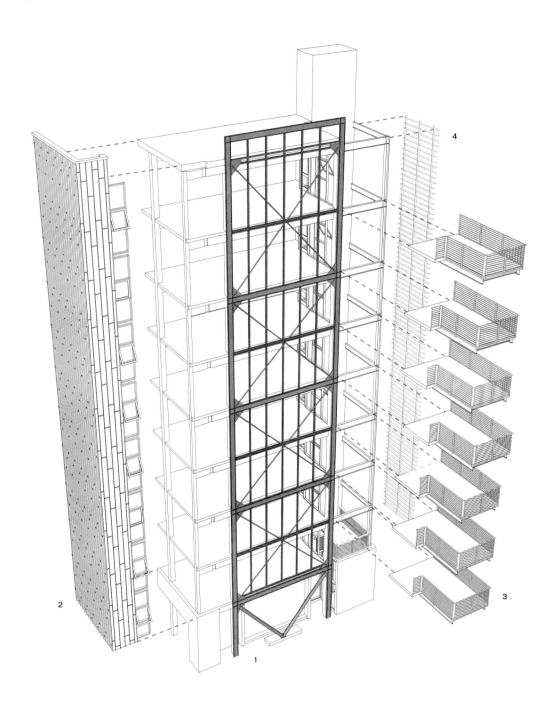

drawing shows the building's structural and enclosure systems. Key: (1) The steel cross bracing (carrying lateral loads) and subframe (carrying gravity loads) provides an armature for the balcony "trays." There is thermal separation between the two steel systems, allowing the expression of the lateral frame on the building exterior without transmitting the temperature differential to the building interior. (2) The opaque metal skin and the steel frame and provides a durable facade facing the alley. (3) Balconies were articulated as lightweight "trays" and project beyond the face of the building to allow views for each unit down the street. These outdoor rooms provide the ability for each unit to naturally ventilate by opening up rear windows and balcony openings. (4) Steel grating provides privacy for the exterior balconies, while allowing for more daylight and filtered views.

Above: Chicago's rich architectural history is on display from every unit within the building.

Left: The building is situated within a growing neighborhood of smaller-scale brick and midrise buildings.

Far left: The building's street elevation was studied using physical models.

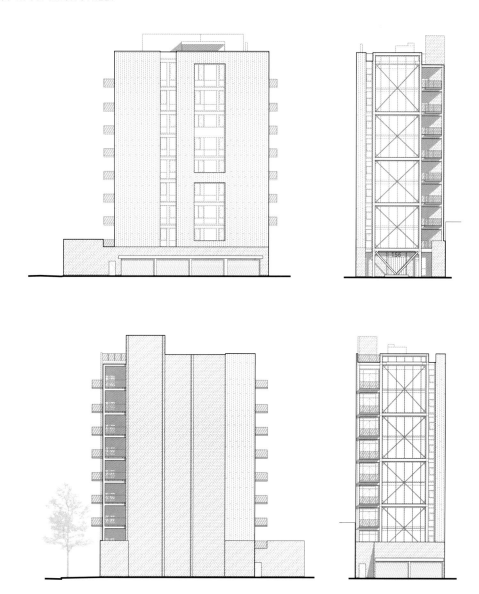

Opposite: The exposed structure, full-height glazing, and exterior balconies clearly describe the organization of the building and spaces within.

Above: Clockwise from top: West, South, North, and East elevations

Following spread: Commercial and industrial products used for stairs and windows as well as in the kichens provide durability, but they also feel light and airy in the building's interior.

Above: Chicago's rich architectural history provided a fertile ground for an exploration into urban housing, here visible from the roof deck.

Above left: Bathroom interior views.

Above right, top: Dave Miller near the exterior balcony screen wall. At the time of construction, a large building was anticipated to the east, so the team developed the steel grating to provide the sense of enclosure for the decks but still allow filtered views.

Above, bottom right: North facade.

Above: The open design of the balcony railing allows unobstructed views from the interior, especially from a sitting sightline, putting the art of their urban fabric on display in each unit.

Opposite: The open and fully glazed character of the street facade allows residential life to be a visible part of the building's street presence.

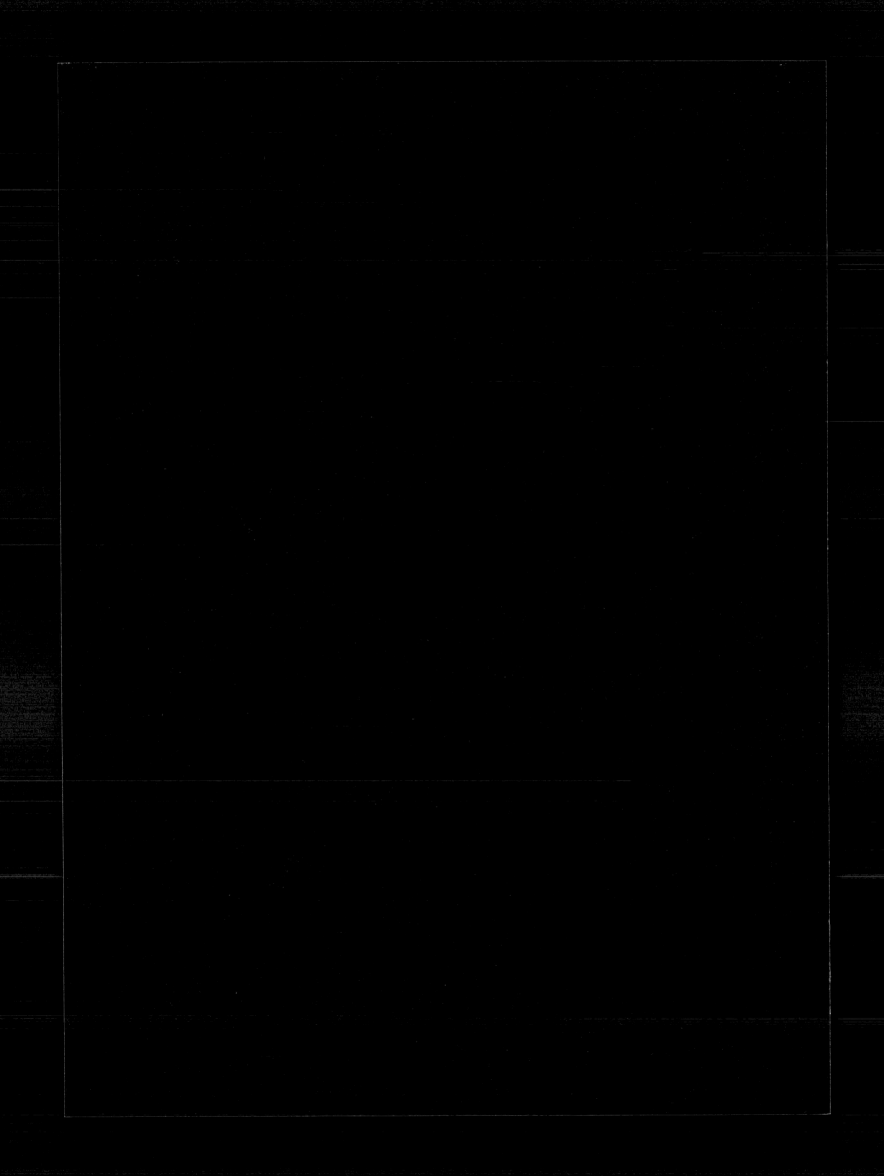

APPENDIX

CONVERSATIONS: MILLER | HULL... *UNPLUGGED*

Editor's note: *John Cava, Brian Carter, and the four original partners of Miller/Hull (Craig Curtis, David Miller, Robert Hull, and Norman Strong) gathered in Seattle in late 2007 to discuss design and cultural philosophies that are an essential part of the way the firm practices architecture. Brian helped moderate the discussion as a way to formulate thoughts for the essays that would ultimately appear in this monograph. The manner in which Miller/Hull practices—via a studio-like collaborative culture—is as essential to us as the end product. The candid studio photographs interspersed throughout this conversation speak to Miller/Hull's informal yet vibrant culture.*

COLLABORATION

BRIAN CARTER: *There aren't many architects practicing in America who are doing public work. In fact, you might say that a considerable amount of American architecture today is figurative and self-referential. How does Miller/Hull see its work in this context?*

NORM STRONG: We work collaboratively, especially on the larger projects, where the systems need to be integrated to make them perform successfully. As a result of that focus, the figurative object seems less important. I hope that when people see our work, they notice the clear expression of program elements, building systems, or conceptual ideas—rather than a self-referential formal statement.

DAVID MILLER: There are some things we have consistently done through the years. For instance: the design gesture with a singular "optimized" form. However, this doesn't always translate to a larger scale. It's more likely that a larger building will be made up of a series of elements that are linked. That is a different strategy, and it's a different way of thinking.

BC: *When you are planning a house or a cabin, is it easier to develop integrated systems than it is for larger projects? Or perhaps you have other aspirations for those larger projects?*

DM: The idea of "stripping away" and making the systems recognizable is consistent in our work.

JOHN CAVA: Miller|Hull has an understanding about the aspect of scale that

is more present in these larger public buildings. It has to do with the firm's philosophy. They are not so inclined to cover everything up with a skin. They are romantics who are also interested in technology, and this brings the focus on engineering. The expression of technology helps us develop ideas of scale, which become more important as the buildings get larger. Perhaps this characteristic in Miller|Hull's work is a result of working on smaller projects where details are experienced at a human scale.

DM: One of the ways we deal with scale is to make buildings legible. In this context the detail is important to us, although there aren't a lot of special details in our work. We work with regular systems, we don't invent them, mainly because our clients don't have the budgets for that. We tend to incorporate off-the-shelf items but use them in a unique way.

ROBERT HULL: Speaking of legibility, one thing that bothers me is putting too many things into a building. That may be a consequence of LEED (Leadership in Energy and Environmental Design) specifications.

For instance, you can get LEED certification for photovoltaics here, bicycle racks there, an earth roof and rainwater collection somewhere else. It's as bad as the old solar days. There |is certainly a preoccupation with adding things in a building that makes for a lack of clarity.

BC: *When you talk about the need for integration on those larger projects, things must be different from when you started the firm in 1977. For example, the three of you could sit down and talk about a house, because the siting, materials, and structural and mechanical systems were all comprehensible.*

NS: When I joined Bob and Dave in the late seventies, there was true collaboration. But over the years, in response to larger projects and a larger staff, "collaboration" has transformed into something else. There is a singular design author for each project, but the idea of one person doing it all is just not feasible.

RH: The presence of individual superstar architects out there is surely stirring things up. Now everybody expects to be wowed and led off in a

new direction by a project. There's certainly a more informed building group out there as a result. Clients expect to be challenged. One of the questions that always strikes terror in me is, "Where's the wow factor?" It's a familiar question, yet I find it a horrible one. Nevertheless, people expect a response.

PURPOSE

BC: *I'm very interested in the nature of practice. It seems generally that "practice" in the United States is very specialized in particular building types. This doesn't happen so much in Europe, and consequently the architect's relationship to other professions is different there than it is in the United States. That being said, is there a way you want to project "practice," not just as Miller/Hull but "practice" across the country?*

NS: We use the phrase "big D, little b," meaning "big Design, little business." The business motivations of the firm definitely take second place. Actually, they probably take fourth place to design! We're not motivated by profits and business aspects, but we're also not embarrassed about making some money and being compensated for what we do. As an architect, you used to be able to roll out a piece of flimsy, take a pencil and a parallel rule, and design. But now the use of technology like building information modeling has transformed practice. We use an interesting mix of tools in our firm today. We still draw by hand and make physical models, but now we have added a laser cutter and other digital tools like BIM, for example. These tools make a difference in how we study projects and how we design.

RH: We started out with projects that had very limited budgets. As a consequence, we became interested in assembling the building in an economic way. I like the utilitarian aspect of our projects. There's a certain kind of pride in producing high-quality work with fairly modest budgets, and we've done that successfully. Money has obviously affected our projects and our design approach—but in a unique way: we use money judiciously.

BC: *In terms of looking forward, let's talk more about aspirations.*

CRAIG CURTIS: Personally, I have quite a bit at stake with that one word. It's the future of our firm. Where do we go? We have the founding partners, who in ten years won't be spending as much time on projects as they are now. Where will the firm be then? Who is going to be picking up the slack here and doing the design work to keep that consistency? Part of the aspiration for this book, in fact, is keeping us at the top of our game and pushing ourselves forward.

RH: The future talent will come from within the firm for sure. We have plenty of good young designers at Miller|Hull, people who can take on challenging and exciting projects.

DM: The conversations about what is appropriate, what kind of materials to use, what are the issues around a project that we should address, and so on—these come out of our set of shared values and attitudes toward our environment. For instance, making the world a better place by design is something that is not often talked about these days, but it means a lot to us.

CC: Conversations about design are a fundamental part of Miller|Hull's studio culture. We still pin up a project for the whole office to discuss every week, which is very helpful. It is definitely harder to focus in a group of fifty or sixty, rather than one of twelve or fifteen. We have made some adjustments as the firm has grown larger so we can still have those types of discussions.

NS: From the firm's beginning, there has been a sense of design without ego. In the future I hope people continue to see Miller|Hull as a forward-thinking firm without a lot of egos. For me, being forward thinking is more about the efforts of the collective group. I would love to have people walk by our projects and say, "That's a Miller|Hull project and it's very good," without having to talk about the individual designer.

DM: I don't think we're necessarily shy about doing iconic buildings, though, but purpose tends to be more important to us.

RH: Our definition of "purpose" would be steeped in sustainability and risk. If you look back at our work from twenty, thirty years ago you'll see projects that were driven by environmental goals, before sustainability became a household word. Don't roll your eyes, but we're interested in making the world a better place. That's a good goal, especially right now, when we're on the verge of losing it.

CC: Our approach to sustainable design is to go beyond green buildings. We try to change behavior by creating spaces that people enjoy. To us, beautiful buildings are inherently about sustainability. Environmental concerns are just another critical part of good design—much like scale or functionality.

BC: *That's a positive role for the firm to take up.*

CC: The project we designed in Scottsdale (A), for example, represents a risk for us. We had many discussions about high-end condominiums in the middle of the desert. There's a limited amount of water there, and we didn't want to add to the problem. However, by designing a project that is dense and by integrating energy-saving and water-conservation features, it becomes an example for future developments. The people who are involved in the project came to understand that it is possible in that kind of setting to be sustainable and still meet the development goals. The client even traded in his Audi for a Prius!

DM: Our work on cabins has also given us license to take risks (B). People say, "Okay, I have my house in the city and it needs to do all these things. But when I go to the island, I want to be challenged and have a place that is stripped down to the basics." The clients have encouraged us to take these risks and challenge them. I remember one client saying, "I really like this idea, but I'm not sure I'm brave enough to do it in my cabin."

RH: That particular idea was to have no roof!

DM: All kidding aside, our cabin clients have given us license to take risks, which we have enjoyed. I think

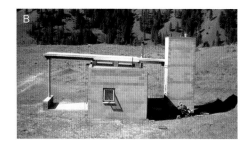

we have also taken that attitude to bigger projects with corporate clients or universities.

RH: Going back to the word "aspiration," I think in our future we need to take more risks. But I think we can do it in the context of how we are trying to make this a better place—the future of the environment and architecture are all wrapped into one.

EVOLUTION

BC: *Nowadays, when you travel, there are essential things to carry, as we don't always check large suitcases anymore. What does Miller/Hull carry forward, from this smaller-scale work into bigger projects?*

RH: How are we making the jump between the small projects and the large ones? That's a good question. We certainly see this as a challenge. What we're looking for is how to maintain the simplicity of the idea in a bigger building. That's not so easy, because the issues and the programs are so much more complex. The Gorton/Bounds (C) cabin is a good example of how a small project helped

develop an idea for a much larger commercial project: Boeing Cafeteria (D). On the cabin we organized all the utility functions into a rectangular "core" along the back of the building. In contrast to this solid building element, the main living spaces were characterized by exposed structure and floor-to-ceiling glass with views out to the water. With Boeing, there were obviously more complex utility spaces and systems required to run a commercial cafeteria. However, the program allowed a very similar plan of organization and building expression. Solid utility spaces were grouped all along one side of the building, and the open, expansive eating area was expressed much like the living space of the cabin.

CC: We strive to make our public buildings accomplish the same things that our houses and cabins do. We're not just trying to solve problems or create iconic architecture—it's much more about the experience that you have when you're living or working in those buildings. Designing houses connects the architect and the client very directly and personally. We strive to make this close relationship happen on the bigger public projects. With

the Kitsap County Administration Building, for example, we tried to design the ideal building both for the people who work there and for the people who come to get information, pay taxes, or file a permit. When I walked through the completed building with the facilities manager, it was as if he were giving a tour of his own home. As an architect, that gives you the ultimate sense of satisfaction.

RH: Whether you walk into a cabin or a big university building, you're the same person. I like to keep that in mind because people sometimes think that they should be or need to be treated in one way when they're in a cabin, but then be provided with fully serviced, air-conditioned spaces in a larger building. When we design, we try to get people to reconsider the need for pervasive or obligatory technical services. For example, you only need complex services for those portions of the building occupied by the actual labs. In all other spaces, we've omitted the air-conditioning where we could and enabled people to open and close windows. This helps to break down the barrier between the serviced building and the real world outside.

INFLUENCES

BC: *You've mentioned before that the time spent working for the Peace Corps was a fundamental influence for both Bob and Dave early on—and translates to how the firm practices today. However, we haven't talked much about influential architects or mentors that have been meaningful to you over the past thirty or forty years.*

DM: Back in school in the sixties, I was fascinated by architecture and media. At the time it was pretty low-tech stuff. I was also influenced by the groundbreaking experimental art and architecture collectives such as Archigram, the Ant Farm, and the Metabolists in Japan. I think that kind of conceptual thinking is still relevant today. The Peace Corps (E) also made a huge impact on me, as well as for Bob. And of course the *Whole Earth Catalog*.

RH: The *Whole Earth Catalog* was a precursor of what we're dealing with today in terms of the focus on natural resources and energy usage. In addition, it was a fantastic collection of ideas, many of which could be implemented, especially around

passive solar and thermal storage. From this standpoint it was really thirty years ahead of its time. Since we opened our office in 1977, energy has been constantly gnawing at the fabric of culture. First you couldn't get gasoline for your car, and now it's damaging the planet.

DM: Bob and I were in an architectural engineering program at Washington State University, so we were taking courses with both civil and mechanical engineering students. We were all indoctrinated to think about how the systems work in our buildings and how they fold into the architecture. As a result, we were drawn more to those kinds of people than the New York Five, who were known more for formalism and less about futuristic concepts.

RH: I was also very influenced by Louis Kahn. I went all over the world to see his and other architects' work, but even then I thought that the great architects tried hard to understand the place where they were working. They understood basic ideas about how site, culture, and environment can influence architecture. These were the same ideas that rung true during

my time in the Peace Corps. Our work there utilized indigenous materials and structures. I would also say these projects were influenced by the Kahn buildings I visited in Bangladesh and India around the same time.

CC: I joined the firm in '87, so I would have to say that my design philosophy has been developed here over the past twenty years with Bob and Dave. Now we have younger people in the office who are stepping up to the plate and helping the firm get to the next level. We are building on what we do well and bringing that forward.

SPIRIT

BC: *Your firm often mentions "spirited architecture." Now that you've been in practice for more than thirty years, do you feel that you've been able to cultivate projects or clients that also seek this? Do you ever turn down projects because they aren't a good match with these values?*

DM: We do not often turn down work, but we are uncomfortable with extravagance. Patagonia, for example, and ECONET (F) (a naturopathic pharmaceutical company) are both clients that fit

our DNA. Our clients at universities, community centers, or library systems often desire an architecture that avoids an impression of luxury.

JC: This highlights another particular aspect of Miller|Hull and its architecture: a notion of everyday modernism.

RH: "Utilitarian" is another word I like to describe our work.

NS: The smaller projects have a spirit of timelessness, openness, innovation, and clarity of purpose that you can feel when you walk through them. More recent larger projects, like the Wilsonville Water Treatment Plant, also have that spirit. That project could have been nothing, just a basic industrial facility, but it has a distinct feeling as you walk through it. It makes a civic gesture.

LANDSCAPE

BC: *Your projects strongly engage the landscape. Is that a function of the dramatic building locations or the firm's conceptual approach to siting the building?*

CC: We take a lot of care in how our buildings respond to landscape. The site is typically a generator for the building concept. That perspective, I think, comes out of the residential work Miller|Hull does. The cabins we do for clients are often their getaway to a place that is more in touch with the site, the view, and so on. This desire to have very strong indoor-outdoor connections, and to look beyond the walls, tends to cross-pollinate our other work.

BC: *The Pierce County Environmental Services Building and the Wilsonville Water Treatment Plant are part of much bigger landscapes. In these instances you are not just designing the site plan for the building; you are responsible for making landscapes.*

CC: You're correct. It's also true with our more urban sites. For instance, on the Northgate Library and Community Center (G), the original site was over three acres of asphalt including a former tire shop—and we turned it into a neighborhood center. That was a project in which we were not dealing with a particularly attractive site, and the neighborhood had developed over

decades without much thought to an identity or center. We created that "heart" in order to knit the surrounding neighborhood together.

OPENINGS

BC: *Many of the firm's projects are characterized by large operable doors or walls, which blend together the interior architecture and surrounding exterior spaces. Could you talk a little bit about how these openings are a part of your conceptual design?*

RH: Opening a window starts to set up all sorts of relationships to the size and the thickness and the thinness of the building. You can't just open a window. You need to have a strategy behind it to make sure that when you do open it, you're going to get air moving through. In turn, that can start to inform the design of a building.

DM: This goes back to the question about the architectural luggage we take to every project. We've always seen an opportunity around making openings. During the design process, Bob looks at what we can do to make an opening a participatory event. It's not just about how it opens the room, but about how a person takes hold of a window, manipulates it, and transforms the room in the process.

BC: *If you think in terms of an office building, the design of a window can take on different but equally potent qualities. If somebody is going to open that window, for example, then is there somebody else who is not able to open it? Traditionally, in an air-conditioned office building the senior managers are along the outside wall and the windows become status symbols. Now, if you have a naturally ventilated office building, suddenly those same people may end up in the middle of the building, and the people who open the windows are the plebes. Is there a committee that calls for everybody to put their hand up when they want fresh air?*

NS: A lot of the projects we design are more for the common good than individual needs. That's one of the strengths of the firm's public work or what we have called "social architecture." By "common good" and "social architecture," I mean we truly enjoy creating spaces that are used by everyone equally within the community versus a single corporation or

individual client. The same goes for the individual—control of his or her own environment while working or living in a space is very important to us as we design.

JC: Another strength of the firm's buildings is that they come alive when people use them.

RH: Our design for the Fort Vancouver Regional Library (H), for example, adds another layer to a traditional library by transforming the way the building works. It's less about the physical size of the building—it's more about how it involves people and about how the whole community will experience it. We've even seen people occupy spaces in ways we never expected, solely because they enjoy the experience. For example, the client of our Environmental Services Building told us recently that residents have started renting the lobby for weddings! That was definitely not something we programmed for: it has evolved due to the experience of the building and its site. We hope all our public work is enjoyed to this degree.

GROWTH

BC: *Do you want the firm to grow?*

RH: I don't know if we've grappled well with the word "growth."

DM: Bob is right. You don't find time to have conversations—about growth, for instance—except when we do a book. We should do a book every year!

NS: We do talk about the size of the firm, but the bottom line is that we think it is important to invest in and be a part of our community. So within the context of a single Miller/Hull office located in Seattle, we need to continue to do more with the great people we have in Seattle on a local, national, and international basis. Toward this end, we've been incorporating more out-reach into our office culture, like our legacy trips to volunteer for the Columbia Land Trust (I, J) or our time dedicated to the 1% solution program.

DM: Growth can be measured in number of staff or in terms of profes-sional exploration. To me, a reason

to be interested in growing might be to enable us to take on larger or more complex commissions with a client or project that would be a challenge for us. Our interest in public work—specifically how these projects can create meaningful experiences for people—is something we'd like to spread to many other kinds of project types and scales.

JC: So it has nothing to do with constraining but rather with focusing your energy so that what you are interested in doing starts to come back to you?

RH: We want to design other kinds of buildings, but at the same time we have the experience to design the buildings we're doing and really extend our potential.

CC: We have some general parameters of where we want to go but how many, where they are, whether they are houses or museums—who knows?

DM: Think about Picasso—he continually reinvented himself. He didn't do the same thing for fifty years. We have a problem if we look through the crystal ball fifteen years ahead, we're doing the same work in the same way.

NS: Always asking "what's next?" is important.

CHRONOLOGY OF BUILDINGS AND PROJECTS

1977
Warren Residence (1)
Moses Lake, Washington

1979
Cedar Hills Activities
Building (2)
Maple Valley, Washington
—
The Evergreen State College
Activities Building (unbuilt)
Olympia, Washington

1980
University of Washington
Health Sciences Projects
Seattle, Washington
—
Hansen Residence
Moses Lake, Washington

1982
Kimmick Earth Shelter
Residence
Cle Elum, Washington
—
Alki Beach Structures
(competition entry)
Seattle, Washington
—
King County Courthouse
Renovation
Seattle, Washington
—
Mercy Earth Shelter
Residence (3)
Lake Marcel, Washington

1984
Central Park Structures
(competition entry)
Bellevue, Washington

1985
The AWARE Shelter (4)
Juneau, Alaska
—

Washington State Pavilion
(competition entry)
Vancouver, British Columbia

1986
King County/Metro (5)
Environmental Lab
Seattle, Washington

1987
Gorton–Bounds Cabin (6)
Decatur Island, Washington
—
Seattle Central Community
College Marine Technology
Center (7)
Seattle, Washington
—
Metzger Residence
Marysville, Washington
—
Meadowdale Beach Rangers
Residence and Park Structures
Lynnwood, Washington

1988
First Hill Diagnostic (MRI)
Imaging Center
Seattle, Washington
—
Adams Elementary School
Seattle, Washington
—
University of Washington
Athletic Program Offices
(unbuilt)
Seattle, Washington

1989
Washington State University
Food Services Building
Pullman, Washington
—
Bolen Cabin
Decatur Island, Washington

1990
The Evergreen State College Art
Studios Addition (8)
Olympia, Washington
—
Novotny Cabin
Decatur Island, Washington
—
Fadem Residence
Orcas Island, Washington
—
Fisheries Teaching and
Research Facility at the
University of Washington
Seattle, Washington
—
Weissbourd Residence
Bainbridge Island, Washington

1991
Boeing Cafeteria (9)
Tukwila, Washington
—
Velodrome and Bicycle
Museum (unbuilt)
Redmond, Washington
—
Lake Washington United
Methodist Church
Kirkland, Washington
—
Seattle Central Community
College Wood Technology
Facility
Seattle, Washington
—
University of Washington
Henderson Hall Addition
(unbuilt)
Seattle, Washington
—
Jackson Cabin
Decatur Island, Washington
—
Poschman Residence (10)
Orcas Island, Washington

1992
Marquand Retreat (11)
Naches River Valley,
Washington
—
Snake Lake Nature Center
Tacoma, Washington
—
Northaven Assisted Living
Facility
Seattle, Washington
—
Lakeside School Arts Facility
(competition entry)
Seattle, Washington
—
Weaver Bergh Residence
and Studio
Bainbridge Island, Washington
—
St. Thomas School
Medina, Washington

1993
University of Washington (12)
Coaches Boathouse
Seattle, Washington
—
SeaTac Community Center
SeaTac, Washington
—
McCaw Cellular Offices
Kirkland, Washington

1994
Girvin Cabin
Decatur Island, Washington
—
Garfield Community
Center (13)
Seattle, Washington
—
Fire Station No. 8
Bellevue, Washington
—
Red Bark Cabin
Decatur Island, Washington

1995
Olympic College–Shelton
Shelton, Washington
—
Passenger-Only Ferry Terminal
(unbuilt)
Seattle, Washington
—
Roundy Residence at Ebey's
Landing
Coupeville, Washington

1996
Northwest Federal Credit
Union (14)
Seattle, Washington
—
McCollum Park and Ride
Facility
Tacoma, Washington
—
City of Issaquah Community
Center
Issaquah, Washington
—
Camarda Residence
Vashon Island, Washington

Patagonia Worldwide
Distribution Center
Reno, Nevada
—
The Olympic Pavilion (unbuilt)
Atlanta, Georgia

1997
Lake Washington School
District Resource Center
Redmond, Washington
—
Tahoma National Cemetery
Kent, Washington
—
Point Roberts Border
Station (15)
Point Roberts, Washington
—

North Kitsap Transportation
Center
Poulsbo, Washington
—
City Light Headquarters Offices
Seattle, Washington
—
Water Pollution Control
Lab (16)
Portland, Oregon
—
Discovery Park Visitor Center
Seattle, Washington
—
Yaquina Head Visitors Center
Newport, Oregon
—
Hansman Residence
Seattle, Washington
—
Epiphany New School
Seattle, Washington

1998
Campbell Orchard Residence
Entiat, Washington
—
Maury Island Cabin
Maury Island, Washington
—
Michaels–Sisson
Residence (17)
Mercer Island, Washington
—
Roddy–Bale Residence
Bellevue, Washington
—
Fremont Public Association
Seattle, Washington
—
Harborview Teaching and
Research Facility
Seattle, Washington
(consultant to MBT Architects)

1999
Transfer and Recycling
Station (18)
Vashon Island, Washington
—
Office Building 2 Improvements
at the Capitol Campus
Olympia, Washington
—
Seattle Water Lab
Seattle, Washington
—
Dixon Residence
Grande Ronde, Washington

2000
King County Library Service
Center
Issaquah, Washington
—
Bainbridge Island City
Hall (19)
Bainbridge Island, Washington
—
Fisher Pavilion at the Seattle
Center
Seattle, Washington

2001
1310 E. Union Lofts
Seattle, Washington
—
Seattle Academy of Arts and
Sciences Performing Arts
Center
Seattle, Washington
—
Saunders Cabin
Guemes Island, Washington
—
Connor Studio
Vashon Island, Washington

2002
Seattle Academy of Arts and
Sciences Gymnasium (20)
Seattle, Washington
—
Smith Homestead Day Use Area
Tillamook, Oregon
—
Pierce County Environmental
Services Building
University Place, Washington
(in association with Arai/
Jackson Architects and
Planners)

Vashon Island Residence
Vashon Island, Washington
—
Campbell Seattle Residence
Seattle, Washington

2003
Seattle Pacific University
Science Building Phase I (21)
Seattle, Washington
—
Washington State University
Shock Physics Building
Pullman, Washington
—
Wilsonville Water
Treatment Plant
Wilsonville, Oregon
(sub to Montgomery
Watson Harza)
—
Lake Washington
Residence (22)
Mercer Island, Washington

2004
Olympic College–Poulsbo
Poulsbo, Washington
—
Northeast Branch Library
Addition and Renovation
Seattle, Washington
—

Childhaven
Seattle, Washington
—
Merrill Hall at the Center for
Urban Horticulture, University
of Washington
Seattle, Washington
—
University of Washington–
Tacoma
McLaren Building and Cherry
Parkes Building Remodels
Tacoma, Washington
—
Roddy Bale Garage Studio and
Addition (23)
Bellevue, Washington
—
Experience Music Project
Interior Renovation
Seattle, Washington
—
East Campus Plaza at the State
Capitol Campus
Olympia, Washington
(subconsultant to EDAW)
—
Dunnington Residence
Decatur Island, Washington
—
El Nido Residence
Decatur Island, Washington
—
Island Residence
Bainbridge Island, Washington

2005
Kitsap County Administration
Building
Port Orchard, Washington
—
South Lake Union Discovery
Center
Seattle, Washington
—
University of Washington
Conibear Shellhouse and
Athletic Center
Seattle, Washington
—

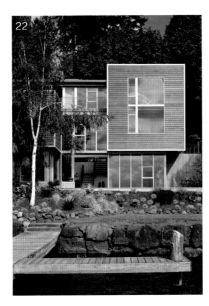

Community Center at
Mercerview (24)
Mercer Island, Washington

—

Nichols-Yeaman Residence
Orcas Island, Washington

—

Tregaron Housing
Development (unbuilt)
Washington, D.C.

—

Hydrogen Futures Park Master
Plan, University of Montana
Futures Park (unbuilt)
Missoula, Montana

—

Boise State University Student
Services Building (unbuilt)
Boise, Idaho

—

Blayney–Myers Residence
Stevens, Washington

—

Huseby Residence
Decatur Island, Washington

2006
Northgate Library, Community
Center, and Urban Park (25)
Seattle, Washington

—

156 W. Superior Street
Chicago, Illinois
(Studio Dwell Architects–
Architect of Record)

—

Bush School
Seattle, Washington

—

Berry–Green Residence
Bainbridge Island, Washington

—

Tillamook Forest Center
Tillamook, Oregon

—

Grand Central Bakery
Portland, Oregon

—

Patagonia PV Installation
Ventura, California

—

Roberts Cabin
Hartstene Island, Washington

—

Econet Corporate Campus
(unbuilt)
Lacey, Washington

2007
Bertschi Center (26)
Seattle, Washington

—

Tacoma Community College
Science and Engineering
Building (27)
Tacoma, Washington

—

Bayley Caretaker's Unit
Seattle, Washington

—

Snoqualmie Branch–King
County Library Services
Community Libraries
Snoqualmie, Washington

—

Orcas Island Cabin
Orcas Island, Washington

—

Pier 59 Renovation and
Reconstruction
Seattle, Washington
(in conjunction with the Seattle
Aquarium Expansion designed
by Mithun)

—

Dinn–Rumley Residence
Grainger, Washington

—

Davis Residence
Bellingham, Washington

2008
Bellevue Community College
Science and Technology
Building
Bellevue, Washington

—

Bethany Church
Expansion (28)
Seattle, Washington

—

North Lake Union Office
Building
Seattle, Washington

—

South Puget Sound Community
College Natural Sciences
Complex
Olympia, Washington

—

Safari Drive Condominiums
(29)
Scottsdale, Arizona

—

Black Diamond Branch–King
County Library Services
Community Libraries
Black Diamond, Washington

—

Carnation Branch–King County
Library Services Community
Libraries (30)
Carnation, Washington

—

Fall City Branch–King County
Library Services Community
Libraries
Fall City, Washington

—

Pier 32 Marina
San Diego, California

—

Marina Green
San Diego, California

2009

Columbia Springs
Environmental Education
Center
Vancouver, Washington
—
Edgewood City Hall (31)
Edgewood, Washington
—
Muckleshoot Branch–King
County Library Services
Community Libraries
Muckleshoot, Washington
—
Technology Access Foundation
Headquarters and Community
Learning Center
White Center, Washington
(in association with Public
Architecture)
—
LOTT Alliance Administration
and Lab Building (32)
Olympia, Washington
—
Northwest Maritime Center
Port Townsend, Washington
—
Kettenburg Marine
San Diego, California
—
Kenton Condominiums
Portland, Oregon
—
Ranquist Residence
Chicago, Illinois
—
Bumber Crop (33)
Scottsdale, Arizona

2010

Engineering and Material
Science Building at the
University of California at
San Diego (34)
La Jolla, California
—
Addition to the School of
Architecture and Planning,
University of Michigan
Ann Arbor, Michigan
—
Redwood Lodge Residential
Community
Mill Valley, California
—
Cascadia Community
College (35)
Global Learning and the Arts
Bothell, Washington

2011

Fort Vancouver Regional
Library (36)
Vancouver, Washington
(in association with Ankrom
Moisan Associated Architects)
—
Seattle Pacific University,
Classroom and Arts Building
Seattle, Washington
—
Galisteo Village (37)
Galisteo Basin, New Mexico

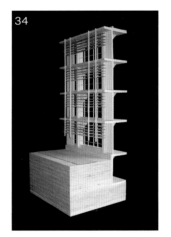

AWARDS

2008

AIA COTE (American Institute
of Architects Committee on the
Environment) Top Ten Awards
South Lake Union Discovery
Center
Seattle, Washington

—

AIA COTE / What Makes It
Green Award
Bertschi Center
Seattle, Washington

—

AISC / IDEAS2 (American
Institute of Steel Construction /
Innovative Design in
Engineering and Architecture
with Structural Steel)
156 W. Superior Street
(condominiums)
Chicago, Illinois

—

Gold Award, Best Sales or Info
Center / Pavilion NAHB
(National Association of Home
Builders)
South Lake Union Discovery
Center
Seattle, Washington

—

Residential Architect
Design Award
156 W. Superior Street
(condominiums)
Chicago, Illinois

—

Honor Award, AIA NW &Pacific
Region, Kitsap County
Administration Building
Port Orchard, Washington

—

The American Architecture
Awards, Chicago Athenaeum
156 W. Superior Street
Chicago, Illinois

—

The American Architecture
Awards, Chicago Athenaeum
Addition to the Art and
Architecture Building,
University of M ichigan
Ann Arbor, Michigan

—

Honor Award, AIA Seattle
Chapter, BumperCrop
Scottsdale, AZ

—

Merit Award, AIA Seattle
Chapter, Kitsap County
Administration Building
Port Orchard, Washington

—

Award of Merit Program,
Olympia Design Review Board
LOTT Alliance Administration
and Lab Building
Olympia, Washington

2007

Merit Award, AIA Northwest
and Pacific Region
156 W. Superior Street
(condominiums)
Chicago, Illinois

—

Sustainable Design Award,
Boston Society of Architects,
Award for Design
South Lake Union Discovery
Center
Seattle, Washington

—

Lifecycle Building Challenge,
Building Category
South Lake Union Discovery
Center
Seattle, Washington

—

Gold Winner, Brick in
Architecture Awards
Northgate Library, Community
Center, and Civic Park
Seattle, Washington

—

Merit Award, AIA Washington
Civic Design Awards
Mercerview Community Center
Mercer Island, Washington

—

Merit Award, AIA Washington
Civic Design Awards
Northgate Library, Community
Center, and Civic Park
Seattle, Washington

—

Merit Award, AIA Washington
Civic Design Awards
Kitsap County Administration
Building
Port Orchard, Washington

—

Governors Tourism
Achievement Award
Tillamook Forest Center
Tillamook, Oregon

—

National AIA Housing
Committee Awards
156 W. Superior Street
(condominiums)
Chicago, Illinois

2006

Excellence in Historic
Preservation, Mayor's Award
Tregaron Residential
Development
Washington, D.C.

—

Award of Merit, AIA Washington
Chapter
156 W. Superior Street
(condominiums)
Chicago, Illinois

—

Honor Award, AIA Washington
Civic Design Awards
University of Washington
Conibear Shellhouse
Seattle, Washington

—

Citation Award, AIA
Washington Civic Design
Awards
University of Washington,
Merrill Hall Reconstruction
Seattle, Washington

—

Honor, Excellence in Concrete
Construction, Washington
Aggregates and Concrete
Construction
East Capitol Campus
Seattle, Washington

—

Citation, Excellence in Concrete
Construction, Washington
Aggregates and Concrete
Construction
University of Washington
Conibear Shellhouse
Seattle, Washington

2005
Merit Award, AIA Southwestern
Washington Design Awards
University of Washington,
Tacoma, Phase 2B Expansion
Tacoma, Washington

—

Honor Award, AIA Northwest
and Pacific Region
Olympic College–Poulsbo
Poulsbo, Washington

—

Citation Award, AIA
Washington Civic Design
Awards
University of Washington,
Tacoma, Phase 2B Expansion
Tacoma, Washington

2004
Award of Merit,
AIA Washington Chapter
Olympic College–Poulsbo
Poulsbo, Washington

—

AIA Business Week/
Architectural Record
Recipient Fisher Pavilion at
the Seattle Center
Seattle, Washington

—

Merit Award, AIA Northwest
and Pacific Region
Fisher Pavilion at the
Seattle Center
Seattle, Washington

—

Merit Award, AIA Northwest
and Pacific Region
Wilsonville Water
Treatment Plant
Wilsonville, Oregon

—

AIA COTE National
Top Ten Green Projects
Pierce County Environmental
Services Building
University Place, Washington

—

EDRA (Environmental Design
Research Association)/
Places Awards Place Design
Wilsonville Water Treatment
Plant
Wilsonville, Oregon

—

Honor Award, AIA Washington
Civic Design Awards
Olympic College–Poulsbo
Poulsbo, Washington

—

Merit Award, AIA Washington
Civic Design Awards
Washington State University,
Shock Physics Institute
Pullman, Washington

2003
AIA National Firm Award

—

Honor Award,
AIA Seattle Chapter
Wilsonville Water
Treatment Plant
Wilsonville, Oregon

—

Honor Award, Masonry
Institute of Washington
Seattle Pacific University,
Phase 1 Science Building
Seattle, Washington

—

AIA COTE National Top Ten
Green Projects
Fisher Pavilion at the Seattle
Center
Seattle, Washington

—

Honor Award, AIA Washington
Civic Design Awards
Fisher Pavilion at the Seattle
Center
Seattle, Washington

—

Grand Award, Concrete
Masonry Institute
Fisher Pavilion at the Seattle
Center
Seattle, Washington

—

Merit Award, AIA Washington
Civic Design Awards
Pierce County Environmental
Services Building
Pierce County, Washington

—

AIA Washington, Housing the
Northwest Award
1310 E. Union Lofts
(mixed-use building)
Seattle, Washington

2002
Merit Award,
AIA Seattle Chapter
Fisher Pavilion at the Seattle
Center
Seattle, Washington

—

Commendation Award,
AIA Seattle Chapter
Seattle Academy Gymnasium
Building
Seattle, Washington

—

The Mayors Institute,
Excellence in City Design
Bainbridge Island City Hall
Bainbridge, Washington
Transfer and Recycling Station
Vashon, Washington

—

Honor Award, AIA Northwest
and Pacific Region
1310 E. Union Lofts (mixed-use
building)
Seattle, Washington

—

Honor Award, AIA Northwest
and Pacific Region
Water Pollution Control
Laboratory
Portland, Oregon

—

Merit Award, AIA Northwest
and Pacific Region
Transfer and Recycling Station
Vashon Island, Washington

—

Seattle Design Commission
Commendation Award
Fisher Pavilion at the Seattle
Center
Seattle, Washington

—

American Institute of Steel
Construction Award
1310 E. Union Lofts
(mixed-use building)
Seattle, Washington

2001
Merit Award, AIA Northwest
and Pacific Region
Bainbridge Island City Hall
Bainbridge, Washington

—

Merit Award,
AIA Seattle Chapter
1310 E. Union Lofts (mixed-use
building)
Seattle, Washington

—

Citation Award, AIA Seattle
Chapter (unbuilt)
Fisher Pavilion at the Seattle
Center
Seattle, Washington

—

Citation Award, AIA Seattle
Chapter
Transfer and Recycling Station
Vashon Island, Washington

2000
Honor Award,
AIA Seattle Chapter
Bainbridge Island City Hall
Bainbridge, Washington

—

Honor Award, AIA Washington
Civic Design Awards
Bainbridge Island City Hall
Bainbridge, Washington

—

Earth Day Top 10 National
Projects / AIA
Bainbridge Island City Hall
Bainbridge, Washington

—

Merit Award, AIA Seattle
Chapter
Roddy–Bale Residence
Bellevue, Washington

—

Honor Award, AIA National
Point Roberts Border Facility
Point Roberts, Washington

—

Honor Award, AIA Northwest
and Pacific Region
Point Roberts Border Facility
Point Roberts, Washington

—

Honor Award, AIA Northwest
and Pacific Region
Ching Cabin
Decatur Island, Washington

—

Merit Award, AIA Northwest
and Pacific Region
Campbell Orchard Residence
Tieton, Washington

1999
Merit Award,
AIA Seattle Chapter
Ching Cabin
Decatur Island, Washington

—

Merit Award, Sunset Magazine
Ching Cabin
Decatur Island, Washington

—

Citation Award, Sunset
Magazine
Michaels–Sisson Residence
Mercer Island, Washington

—

Citation Award, Sunset
Magazine
Marks Residence
Vashon Island, Washington

—

Civic Design Award, City
of Redmond
Lake Washington Resource
Center
Redmond, Washington

—

Federal Design Achievement
Award
Point Roberts Border Facility
Point Roberts, Washington

—

Honor Award, AIA National
Olympic College–Shelton
Shelton, Washington

—

Honor Award, AIA
Northwest and Pacific Region
Michaels–Sisson Residence
Mercer Island, Washington

—

Honor Award ASLA
(American Society of
Landscape Architects),
National Water Pollution
Control Laboratory
Portland, Oregon

—

Commendation Award,
AIA Seattle Chapter
Yaquina Head Interpretive
Center
Newport, Oregon

1998
Earth Day Top Ten National
Projects / AIA
Patagonia Distribution Center
Reno, Nevada

—

Honor Award, AIA National
Olympic College–Shelton
Shelton, Washington

—

General Services
Administration, Honor Award
for Design Excellence
Point Roberts Border Facility
Point Roberts, Washington

—

Honor Award, AIA, Seattle
Chapter
Point Roberts Border Facility
Point Roberts, Washington

—

Honor Award, AIA, Seattle
Chapter
Michaels–Sisson Residence
Mercer Island, Washington

—

Merit Award,
AIA Seattle Chapter
Campbell Orchard Residence
Tieton, Washington

—

Citation Award,
AIA Seattle Chapter
Water Pollution Control
Laboratory
Portland, Oregon

—

Honor Award, American
Wood Council
Ching Cabin
Decatur Island, Washington

—

Citation Award, American
Wood Council
Discovery Park Visitor Center
Seattle, Washington

—

Merit Award, AIA Northwest
and Pacific Region
Discovery Park Visitor Center
Seattle, Washington

—

Best New Public Building,
Oregon Concrete
and Aggregate Producers
Association and Oregon
Chapter American Concrete
Institute Yaquina Head
Interpretive Complex
Newport, Oregon

—

Citation Award, Conceptual,
AIA Seattle Chapter
Grande Ronde Residence
Grande Ronde, Washington

—

Best of Program Award,
National CMA/AIA
Campbell Orchard Residence
Tieton, Washington

—

Commendation Award,
AIA Seattle Chapter
Water Pollution Control
Laboratory
Portland, Oregon

—

Special Mention Award,
Laboratory of the Year
Program, Research &
Development Magazine
Water Pollution Control
Laboratory
Portland, Oregon

1997
Sustainable Design Award,
Boston Society of Architects
Patagonia Distribution Center
Reno, Nevada

—

Merit Award, Portland General
Electric's Energy User News
Water Pollution Control
Laboratory
Portland, Oregon

—

Merit Award for Stormwater
Design, Metro of Portland
Water Pollution Control
Laboratory
Portland, Oregon

—

Merit Award, BPA
Architecture + Energy
Water Pollution Control
Laboratory
Portland, Oregon

—

Merit Award, AIA Northwest
and Pacific Region
Camarda Residence
Vashon Island, Washington

—

Honor Award, Sunset Magazine
Island Cabin
Decatur Island, Washington

—

Merit Award, Sunset Magazine
Camarda Residence
Vashon Island, Washington

—

Citation Award, Sunset
Magazine
Hansman Residence
Seattle, Washington

—

Merit Award,
AIA Seattle Chapter
Discovery Park Visitor Center
Seattle, Washington

—

Merit Award, Best Projects
of the Year, 1997 Construction
Data News Magazine
Yaquina Head Interpretive
Complex
Newport, Oregon

—

Honor Award, AIA Portland
Chapter
Water Pollution Control
Laboratory
Portland, Oregon

—

Honor Award, Interior Design
Associates, Portland
Water Pollution Control
Laboratory
Portland, Oregon

—

Excellence on the
Waterfront Annual Award
Water Pollution Control
Laboratory
Portland, Oregon

—

Merit Award for New
Construction, ASLA,
Washington
Water Pollution Control
Laboratory
Portland, Oregon

—

Safety Award for Ergonomic
Improvements, City of
Portland's Risk
Management Group
Water Pollution Control
Laboratory
Portland, Oregon

—

Extraordinary Use of Public
Funds Award AIA, ASID
(American Society of Interior
Designers), and IIDA
(International Interior Design
Association), Portland Chapters
Water Pollution Control
Laboratory
Portland, Oregon

1996
Commendation Award, AIA
Seattle
Camarda Residence
Vashon Island, Washington

—

Citation Award, BPA
Architecture + Energy
Northwest Federal Credit Union
Seattle, Washington

—

Award of Excellence, Sunset
Magazine
Camarda Residence
Vashon Island, Washington

—

Top Merit Award, AIA / NCMA
(National Concrete Masonry
Association) Design Awards
Marquand Retreat
Yakima, Washington

—

Award for Excellence in
Planning and Design, Record
Houses Design Awards,
Record (April 1996)
Island Cabin
Decatur Island, Washington

—

Citation Award, AIA Seattle
Chapter
Point Roberts Border Station
Point Roberts, Washington

—

Grand Award, AIA Northwest
and Pacific Region
Olympic College–Shelton
Shelton, Washington

1995
Merit Award,
American Wood Council
Olympic College–Shelton
Shelton, Washington

—

Honor Award, AIA Seattle
Chapter
Olympic College–Shelton
Shelton, Washington

—

Home of the Decade Award,
1980–1990
AIA / *Seattle Times* Home
of the Month
Mercy Residence
Lake Marcel, Washington

—

Merit Award, AIA Northwest
and Pacific Region
Island House
Decatur Island, Washington

—

Honor Award, AIA Seattle
Chapter
Garfield Community Center
Seattle, Washington

—

Citation for Future Work, AIA
Portland Chapter
Water Pollution Control Lab
Portland, Oregon

Special Recognition Masonry
Institute of Washington
Garfield Community Center
Seattle, Washington

1994
Citation for Future Work,
AIA Seattle Chapter
Eastern Washington University,
Student Union Addition
Cheney, Washington

—

Merit Award, American Wood
Council of Washington, D.C.
Island Cabin
Decatur Island, Washington

—

Merit Award,
AIA Seattle Island Cabin
Decatur Island, Washington

—

Honor Award, AIA Northwest
and Pacific Region
Marquand Retreat
Yakima, Washington

1993
Honor Award, AIA Seattle
Marquand Retreat
Yakima, Washington

—

Honor Award, AIA Seattle
Weaver–Bergh Residence
Bainbridge Island, Washington

—

Honor Award, AIA Northwest
and Pacific Region
Jackson House
Decatur Island, Washington

—

Merit Award, Drive-by Jury, AIA
Northwest and Pacific Region
Jackson House
Decatur Island, Washington

—

Merit Award, Sunset Magazine
Roundy Residence
Ebey's Landing, Washington

—

Citation Award, Sunset
Magazine
Marquand Retreat
Yakima, Washington

—

Citation Award, Sunset
Magazine
Novotny Cabin
Decatur Island, Washington

—

Honor Award, AIA Northwest
and Pacific Region
Boeing Cafeteria 9-12
Seattle, Washington

—

Award Winner, Cedar Shake
and Shingle Bureau
Lake Washington United
Methodist Church
Kirkland, Washington

—

Award Winner Metal in
Architecture
The Boeing Cafeteria
Seattle, Washington

—

Merit Award, Masonry Institute
of Washington
Adams Elementary School
Seattle, Washington

1992
Honor Award, AIA Northwest
and Pacific Region
Novotny Cabin
Decatur Island, Washington

—

Citation for Future Work, AIA
Seattle
Lakeside School Art Facility
Seattle, Washington

—

Merit Award, ASLA
Meadowdale Beach Park
Lynnwood, Washington

1991
Excellence in Planning and
Design, Record Houses Design
Award, *Record* (April 1991)
Novotny Cabin
Decatur Island, Washington

—

Honor Award, AIA Seattle
Jackson House
Decatur Island, Washington

—

Citation for Future Work, AIA
Seattle
Poschman Residence
Orcas Island, Washington

—

Design Award, American Wood
Council of Washington, D.C.
Novotny Cabin
Decatur Island, Washington

—

Honor Award, AIA Northwest
and Pacific Region
Novotny Cabin
Decatur Island, Washington

—

Daily Journal of Commerce/
AIA Seattle
July Project of the Month
University of Washington
Fisheries Teaching and
Research Building
Seattle, Washington

—

Merit Award,
AIA Seattle Chapter
Boeing Cafeteria 9-12
Seattle, Washington

—

Honor Award, AIA Northwest
and Pacific Region
Marine Technology Facility
Seattle, Washington

1990
Merit Award, AIA Seattle
Novotny Cabin
Decatur Island, Washington

—

Merit Award, *Sunset Magazine*
Bolen Cabin
Decatur Island, Washington

—

Merit Award, AIA Seattle
Bolen Cabin
Decatur Island, Washington

—

Citation Award, AIA Seattle
Chapter
Future Project, Seattle
Passenger-Only Ferry Terminal
Seattle, Washington

—

Merit Award,
AIA Seattle Chapter
Future Project, Charles Street
Maintenance Facility
Seattle, Washington

—

Merit Award, ASLA
Meadowdale Beach Park
Lynnwood, Washington

1989
Merit Award, Sunset Magazine
Bolen Cabin
Decatur Island, Washington

—

People's Choice Award,
AIA Seattle
Bolen Cabin
Decatur Island, Washington

—

Merit Award, ASLA
Meadowdale Beach Park
Lynnwood, Washington

—

Merit Award, AIA Seattle
Chapter, Evergreen State
College, Art Studios Addition
Olympia, Washington

1987
Honor Award, *Sunset Magazine*
Gorton–Bounds Cabin
Decatur Island, Washington
—

Merit Award, *Sunset Magazine*
Metzger Residence
Lake Marcel, Washington
—

Honor Award, AIA Seattle
Marine Technology Facility
Seattle, Washington
—

High Honor Award, National
Lab of the Year, Metro
Environmental Laboratories
Seattle, Washington
—

Honor Award,
AIA Seattle Chapter
Marine Technology Facility
Seattle, Washington

1986
Honor Award and People's
Choice Award,
AIA Seattle Chapter, Metro
Environmental Laboratories
Seattle, Washington

1985
Honor Award, American Wood
Council of Washington D.C.
The Aware Women's Shelter
Juneau, Alaska
—

Honor Award, AIA Seattle
and People's Choice Award
The Aware Women's Shelter
Juneau, Alaska
—

Honor Award, AIA Seattle
Gorton–Bounds Cabin
Decatur Island, Washington
—

People's Choice Award,
AIA Seattle
Gorton–Bounds Cabin
Decatur Island, Washington

1983
Honor Award, Sunset Magazine
Mercy Residence
Lake Marcel, Washington
—

Citation Award, American
Wood Council
Cedar Hills Activities Building
Maple Valley, Washington

1982
Honor Award, AIA Seattle
Cedar Hills Activities Building
Maple Valley, Washington
—

Honor Award, AIA Seattle
Mercy Residence
Lake Marcel, Washington
—

AIA Home of the Month
Mercy Residence
Lake Marcel, Washington
—

Citation of Merit, National
Plywood Design Awards
Cedar Hills Activities Building
Maple Valley, Washington
—

Merit Award, AIA Seattle
Chapter, Future Project,
Charles Street Maintenance
Facility
Seattle, Washington

1980
Finalist Award, The Fifth
National Passive Solar
Competition
Kimmick Residence
Cle Elum, Washington
Hansen Residence
Moses Lake, Washington

PROJECT DATA

SOUTH LAKE UNION DISCOVERY CENTER
Seattle, Washington

—

Building area: 11,000 square feet
Project team: David Miller, Bill Franklin,
    Ruth Coates, Petra Michaely, Chris Armes,
    Dustin Stephens, Doug Mikko
Client: Vulcan Real Estate
Structural engineer: Magnusson Klemencic
    Associates
Civil engineer: Magnusson Klemencic Associates
Mechanical engineer: University Mechanical
Electrical engineer: Cochran Electric
Lighting design: Candela
Landscape architect: Brumbaugh & Associates
Interiors: Mice Marketcraft
General contractor: GLY Construction
Completion date: 2005

TECHNOLOGY ACCESS FOUNDATION
HEADQUARTERS AND COMMUNITY
LEARNING CENTER
White Center, Washington

—

Building area: 24,155 square feet
Project team: Craig Curtis, Norman Strong,
    Doug Mikko, Caroline Kreiser, Evan
    Bourquard, Molly Cooper, Jim Hanford,
    Elizabeth Moggio, in association with
    Public Architecture
Client: Technology Access Foundation
Structural engineer: Bright Engineering
Civil engineer: SvR
Mechanical engineer: Greenbusch
A/V and acoustical: Greenbusch
Electrical engineer: CB Engineers
Landscape architect: SvR
Costing: Robinson
General contractor: to be determined
Kitchen Consultant: Clevenger & Associates
Interior design: 33Design
Completion date: estimated 2010

WILSONVILLE WATER TREATMENT PLANT
Wilsonville, Oregon

—

Project team: Robert Hull, Sian Roberts, Joyce Too
Client: City of Wilsonville
Contractor: Montgomery Watson Harza
Design build: Encompasses Civil, Structural,
    Mechanical, Electrical, Costing:
Landscape architect: Murase Associates
Completion date: 2003

TILLAMOOK FOREST CENTER
Tillamook, Oregon

—

Building area: 14,300 square feet
Project team: Robert Hull, Craig Curtis, Amy
    Dedominicis, Teresa Russell, Molly Cooper,
    Huyen Hoang, Claudine Manio
Client: Oregon Department of Forestry
Structural engineers: Tetra/Tech / Kcm, Inc.
Civil engineers: Tetra/Tech / Kcm, Inc.
Mechanical engineers: PAE Consulting
    Engineers, Inc.
Electrical engineers: PAE Consulting
    Engineers, Inc.
Lighting consultant: Luma Lighting Design
Acoustical: Listen Acoustics
Interpretive design: Aldrich Pears Associates
Sustainable design: O'Brien & Company
Interior design: Allbee Romein
Costing: Roen and Associates
Landscape architect: Walker Macy
General contractor: Precision Construction
    Company
Bridge consultant: Weyerhaeuser
Consultant: Breshears/Thornton Consultants
Completion date: 2006

PIERCE COUNTY ENVIRONMENTAL
SERVICES BUILDING
University Place, Washington
—

Building area: 49,810 square feet
Project team: Craig Curtis, Scott Wolf, Rob
    Hutchison, Petra Michaely, Sian Roberts,
    Joyce Too, Boaz Ashkenazy, in association
    with Arai/Jackson Architects & Planners
Client: Pierce County Public Works & Utilities
Structural engineers: AHBL
Civil engineers: SvR Design Co.
Mechanical engineers: AE Associates
Electrical engineers: J Omega
Acoustical: The Greenbusch Group
Interpretive design: Aldrich Pears Associates
Construction management: Olympic Associates
Kitchen consultant: Chandler/Wilson Design
Landscape architect: Bruce Dees & Associates
General contractor: Wick Constructors, Inc.
Costing: Roen and Associates
Completion date: 2002

KITSAP COUNTY ADMINISTRATION
BUILDING
Port Orchard, Washington
—

Building area: 75,376 gross square feet
Project team: Craig Curtis, Sian Roberts,
    Robert Misel, Petra Michaely, Tim Politis,
    Kim Shiell, Anne Seaton, Chris Armes,
    Joy Rubey, Thomas Brown
Client: Kitsap County Department of
    Administrative Services
Structural engineers: AHBL
Civil engineers: SvR Design Co.
Mechanical engineers: TAC (formerly Abacus)
Electrical engineers: TAC (formerly Abacus)
Signage: Jon Bentz Design
Waterproofing: Wetherholt
Acoustical: BRC
Landscape architect: Site Workshop
Geotech. engineer: Myers Biodynamics
Hardware: Adams Consulting
Specifications writer: Specifications Northwest
General contractor: Swinerton Builders
Costing: Roen and Associates
Completion date: 2005

FISHER PAVILION AT THE SEATTLE CENTER
Seattle, Washington
—

Building area: 24,000 square feet
Project team: Robert Hull, Ron Rochon, Scott
    Wolf, Ruth Coates, Margaret Sprug, Pat Byrne,
    Steve Tatge, Steve Southerland, Claudine
    Manio, Mark Adams
Client: City of Seattle, Seattle Center
Structural engineers: AKB Engineers
Civil engineers: AKB Engineers
Mechanical engineers: The Greenbusch Group
Electrical engineers: Sparling, Inc.
Acoustical: The Greenbusch Group
Landscape architect: Siteworkshop
Costing: Robinson Company
General contractor: Howard S. Wright
    Construction Co.
Completion date: 2002

OLYMPIC COLLEGE–POULSBO
Poulsbo, Washington
—

Building area: 40,000 square feet
Project team: Norman Strong, Craig Curtis,
    Scott Wolf, Ruth Coates, Bill Franklin,
    Amy Dedominicis, Rob Hutchinson, Daniel
    Mihalyo, Annie Han, Laurie Fanger
Client: Olympic College
Structural engineer: AKB Engineers
Civil engineer: AKB Engineers
Mechanical engineer: The Greenbusch Group
Electrical/lighting: Sparling
Low voltage/data: Sparling
Landscape architect: EDAW/Siteworkshop
Specifications writer: Specifications Northwest
General contractor: Howard S. Wright
    Construction Co.
Completion date: 2004

UNIVERSITY OF WASHINGTON CONIBEAR
SHELLHOUSE AND ATHLETIC CENTER
Seattle, Washington

—

Building area: 48,092 square feet
Project team: Bob Hull, Norm Strong, Steve
    Southerland, Katie Popolow, Mike Jobes,
    Ruth Coates, Brendan Rose, Huyen Hoang
Client: University of Washington
Structural engineer: Magnusson Klemencic
Civil engineer: Reid Middleton
Mechanical engineer: Keen Engineering
Electrical engineer: Travis Fitzmaurice
Landscape architect: Siteworkshop
Food service: JLR
Interiors: Robin Dalton, LMN
Costing: Davis Langdon Adamson
General contractor: Sellen Construction
Completion date: 2005

ADDITION TO THE ART AND ARCHITECTURE
BUILDING, UNIVERSITY OF MICHIGAN
Ann Arbor, Michigan

—

Building area: 16,350 square feet
Project team: Bob Hull, Ron Rochon, Heidi Oien,
    Elizabeth Moggio, Doug Mikko, John MacKay,
    Michael Henderson
Client: The Regents of the University of Michigan,
    Taubman College of Architecture and Urban
    Planning
Local architect: A3C, Ann Arbor
Structural engineer: Structural Design
    Incorporated
Civil engineer: Professional Engineering
    Associates
Mechanical engineer: PAE Consulting Engineers,
    Inc., Portland, Oregon/MA Engineering,
    Bingham Farms, Michigan
Electrical engineer: PAE Consulting Engineers,
    Inc., Portland, Oregon/MA Engineering,
    Bingham Farms, Michigan
Lighting: Integrated Design Lab
Landscape architect: Professional Engineering
    Associates
Costing: Faithful+Gould
General contractor: to be determined
Completion date: estimated 2010

1310 E. UNION LOFTS
Seattle, Washington

—

Building area: 16,800 square feet
Project team: David Miller, Lene Copeland,
    Kurt Stolle, Brian Court
Client: Anemone, LLC
Structural engineer: Swenson Say Faget
Civil engineer: Taylor Engineering Consultants
Mechanical engineer: Sider & Byers
Landscape architect: Atelier, PS
General contractor: Turner Construction
    Company SPD
Completion date: 2001

156 W. SUPERIOR STREET
Chicago, Illinois

—

Building area: 25,000 square feet
Project team: David Miller, Kurt Stolle, Brian
    Court
Client: Ranquist Development, Inc.
Architect of record: Studio Dwell Architects
Structural engineer: Thornton Tomasetti
    Engineers
General contractor: Skender Construction
    Company
Completion date: 2006

SELECTED BIBLIOGRAPHY

BOOKS
—

Greensource. *Emerald Architecture: Case Studies in Green Building*. New York: McGraw-Hill Construction Publication, 2008.

Kendra Langeteig. *The New Asian Home*. Layton, Utah: Gibbs Smith, 2008.

Kiel Moe. *Integrated Design in Contemporary Architecture*. New York: Princeton Architectural Press, 2008.

Nancy Solomon, AIA. *Architecture: Celebrating the Past, Designing the Future*. New York: Visual Reference Publications, 2008.

Alison Kwok, AIA and Walter Grondzik, PE. *The Green Studio Handbook: Environmental Strategies for Schematic Design*. Oxford: Architectural Press, 2007.

Daniel Williams, FAIA. *Sustainable Design: Ecology, Architecture and Planning*. Hoboken, N.J.: Wiley, 2007.

Panache Partners, ed. *Dream Homes Pacific Northwest: An Exclusive Showcase of the Finest Architects, Designers, and Builders in Oregon and Washington*. Plano, Tex.: Panache Partners LLC, 2007.

Sarah Nettleton. *The Simple Home: The Luxury of Enough*. Newton, Conn.: Taunton Press, 2007.

Alanna Stang and Christopher Hawthorne. *The Green House: New Directions in Sustainable Architecture*. New York: Princeton Architectural Press, 2006.

Jeremiah Eck. *The Face of Home: A New Way to Look at the Outside of Your House*. Newton, Conn.: Taunton Press, 2006.

Marc Vassallo. *The Barefoot Home*. Newton, Conn.: Taunton Press, 2006.

David Miller. *Toward a New Regionalism*. Seattle, Wash.: University of Washington Press, 2005.

Phaidon Press. *Phaidon Atlas of World Architecture*. London: Phaidon Press, 2004.

Nicolas Pople. *Small Houses: Contemporary Residential Architecture*. New York: Universe Publishing, 2003.

Oscar Riera Ojeda, ed. *Forty Houses*. Gloucester, Mass.: Rockport Publishers, 2003.

Images Publishing Group. *One Hundred of the World's Best Houses*. Mulgrave, Victoria, Australia: Images, 2002.

Linda Leigh Paul. *Coastal Retreats—The Pacific Northwest and the Architecture of Adventure*. New York: Rizzoli, 2002.

Max Jacobson, Murray Silverstein, and Barbara Winslow. *Patterns of Home: The Ten Essentials of Enduring Design*. Newton, Conn.: Taunton Press, 2002.

Sheri Olson. *Miller|Hull: Architects of the Pacific Northwest*. New York: Princeton Architectural Press, 2001.

James Grayson Trulove and Il Kim, eds. *The New American Cottage—Innovations in Small-Scale Residential Architecture*. New York: Whitney Library of Design, 1999.

Oscar Riera Ojeda, ed. *Ten Houses: Miller|Hull Partnership*. Gloucester, Mass.: Rockport Publishers, 1999.

Marcie Stuchin and Susan Abramson, eds. *Waterside Homes*. Glen Cove, N.Y.: Rizzoli, 1998.

Peter Zellner, ed. *Pacific Edge: Contemporary Architecture on the Pacific Rim*. New York: Rizzoli, 1998.

Gustau Gili Galfetti, ed. *Casa Refugio* (Private retreats). Barcelona: 1995.

John Carmody and Raymond Sterling, eds. *Earth Sheltered Housing Design*. Minneapolis, Minn.: Van Nostrand Reinhold Company, 1985.

Lance T. Holthusen, ed. *Earth Sheltering: The Form of Energy and the Energy of Form*. New York: Pergamon Press: 1981.

PERIODICALS
—

David Tyda. "Welcome to the Neighborhood." *Desert Living Magazine* (March 2008): 114–19.

Blair Kamin. "156 West Superior Residences." *Architectural Record* (May 2007): 226–29.

Cheryl Weber. "Big and Green." *Residential Architect* (March 2007): 52–55.

Garret Browne. "Squeezed." *Modern Steel Construction* (June 2007): 23–24.

Kira Gould. "Rebirth and Regeneration." *GreenSource Magazine* (November 2006): 72–75.

James Russell. "Olympic College Poulsbo." *Architectural Record* (December 2004): 192–97.

Jane Kolleeny and Audrey Beaton. "Design Solutions That Enhance Business Success." *Business Week* (November 2004): 68.

Jil Peters. "Dream Cabin." *Sunset* (August 2004): 99–103.

Sheri Olson. "Firm of the Year Award: A Spirit of Openness Propels Miller|Hull to Excellence." *Architectural Record* (May 2003): 172–82.

Sheri Olson. "1310 East Union, Miller|Hull's Striking Steel-Framed, Transparent Live/Work Lofts, Sing an Ode to Modernism." *Architectural Record* (October 2002): 229–32.

Paul Makovskyl. "New Architecture Faces the Future." *Metropolis* (April 2000): 75.

Sheri Olson. "Feature Residence: Roddy Bale Residence." *Architectural Record* (July 2000): 204–9.

"American Institute of Architects 1999 Honors and Awards." *Architectural Record* (May 1999): 136.

Mario Caldarelli. "Concavo, convesso—Olympic College Shelton." *L'Arca* (June 1999): 12–17.

Sheri Olson. "Yaquina Head Gives Visitors the Key to a Kingdom by the Sea." *Architectural Record* (October 1999): 144–46.

Vernon Mays. "Northwest Passion." *Residential Architect* (September/October 1999): 52–58, 60, 62.

William Thompson. "The Poetics of Stormwater." *Landscape Architecture* (January 1999): 58–63, 86.

Lawrence W. Cheek. "A Four-Square House by Miller|Hull Partnership Stands Its Ground Beneath a Dense Wooded Canopy." *Architecture* (December 1998): 84–89.

Trevor Boddy. "Border Lines." *Architecture* (May 1998): 140–43.

Mark Hinshaw. "Architecture WaterWorks." *Architecture Magazine* (July 1997): 102–07.

Ruggero Borghi and Martina Botta. "Astrazioni nella natura" (Abstractions in nature). *Ville Giardini* (February 1997): 18–19.

Trevor Boddy. "NW Federal Credit Union, Seattle, Washington." *Architectural Record* (June 1997): 140–43.

William Thompson. "Mail-Order Pride." *Landscape Architecture* (March 1997): 56–61.

A.C.S. "On the Boards. " *Architecture* (October 1996): 56.

"Case Study: Patagonia Building a Model for Green Planning." *Environmental Building News* (September/October 1996): 8–9.

Charles Linn. "Island Retreat Fits Rocky Site." *Architectural Record* (April 1996): 80–83.

Linda O'Keeffe and Linda Humphrey. "The Family Tree House." *Metropolitan Home* (July 1996): 124–25.

Marco Biagi and Marina Botta. "Povera e bella" (Poor and beautiful). *Ville Giardini* (February 1996): 34–37.

Sheri Olson. "A True Community College." *Architectural Record* (November 1996): 90–93.

A.C.S. "On the Boards." *Architecture* (July 1995): 39.

Donald Canty. "Seattle Community Centers Put Sustainability to the Test." *Places* (Winter 1995): 78.

Marco Biagi. "La valle dell' Eden" (The valley of Eden). *Ville Giardini* (June 1995): 28–29.

Mark Hinshaw. "New Public Outlook." *Architecture* (June 1995): 78–83.

"Vitality Wins the Day." *Progressive Architecture* (December 1995): 35.

Justin Henderson. "Retreat into Nature." *Architecture* (May 1994): 88.

———. "Structural Shade." *Architecture* (October 1992): 72–75.

Undine Prohl. "Forsters Wachtturm War Das Vorbild" (Forster's watchtower was the model). *Hauser Magazine* (March 1992): 124–30.

Donald Canty. "Home Alone." *Architectural Record* (April 1991): 122–25.

Dylan Landis. "On the Lookout for a Natural Life: A Cabin in the Sky." *Metropolitan Home* (June 1991): 80–83.

Donald J. Canty. "Regional Portfolio—The Pacific Northwest." *Architectural Record* (May 1990): 88–89.

Paul M. Sachner. "Maritime Maneuvers." *Architectural Record* (February 1989): 118–19.

Undine Prohl. "Ein Durch und Durch Offenes Versteck" (A completely transparent hideout), *Hauser Magazine* (November 1989): 156–59.

Jim Murphy. "An Open Hideaway." *Progressive Architecture* (December 1988): 96–97.

"A Beautifully Spare 'Long House.'" *Architecture Minnesota* (May 1983): 41.

STAFF AND COLLABORATORS

David Miller
Partner

Robert Hull
Partner

Norman Strong
Partner

Craig Curtis
Partner

Sian Roberts
Partner

Ron Rochon
Partner

Scott Wolf
Partner

Ruth Coates
Principal

Mike Jobes
Principal

Margaret Sprug
Principal

Richard Whealan,
Principal

Brian Court
Associate

Susan Kelly
Associate

Doug Mikko
Associate

Katie Popolow
Associate

Robert Misel
Associate

Current Staff
—
David Arnold
John Barton
Evan Bourquard
Susan Boyer
Thomas Brown
Will Caramella
Ben Dalton
Alan Dodson
Adin Dunning
Chi Duong
Jeff Floor
Bill Franklin
Stewart Germain
Daniel Gero
Kiki Gram
Jim Hanford
Michael Henderson
Cassie Hillman
Karen Johnson
Sini Kamppari
Caroline Kreiser
Grace Leong
Barb Thoreson Linde
Marie Ljubojevic
John MacKay
Jay Martin
Elizabeth Moggio
Heidi Oien
Ed Palushock
Maaike Post
James Radcliffe
Rebecca Roberts
Yuki Seda-Kane
Kim Shiell
Erin Silva
Kate Spitzer
Peter Spruance
Alexa Strong
Laura Tudor
Chad Zettle

Former Staff
—
Mark Adams
Carla Allbee
Christopher Armes
Chris Arthur
Deborah Battle

Seth Bender
Kristin Bergman
Renee Boone
Pete Bruner
Dave Brunner
Patrick Byrne
Allison Capen
Camisa Carlson
Christopher Carlson
Victoria Carter
Scheer Chan
Alice Cho Snyder
Anne Christianson
Philip Christofides
Molly Cooper
Susan Cooper
Lene Copeland
Susana Covarrubias
Amy DeDominicis
Steve deKoch
Steve Doub
Kathleen Dutcher
Laura Dye
Jed Edeler
Laurie Fanger
Allan Farkas
John Feit
Jeanette Felix
Margit Gutmair
Gabriel Hadjiani
Laura Hafermann
Annie Han
Huyen Huang
Robert Hutchison
Vanessa Kaneshiro
Chrys Kim
Lisa Kirkendall
Julie Kreigh
Olivier Landa
Katherine Larson
Amy Lelyveld
Claudine Manio
Michael Mariano
Rhonda Mauer
Tom McCollum
Brian McWatters
Petra Michaely
Andrew Michal
Daniel Mihaylo
Sarah Milsow

Tom Morris
Judy Morrissey
Julie Montgomery
Renae Nelson
Christopher Osolin
Christopher Patano
Richard Pearse
Timothy Politis
Jana Rekosh
Brian Rich
Chad Rollins
Kristin Ross
Rebecca Ross
Brendan Rose
Mary Rowe
Stacy Rowland
Joy Ruby
Heather Sabo
David Sachs
Grace Schlitt
Gail Schroeder
Anne Seaton Scott
Cathi Scott
Teresa Shannon
Patrick Sheahan
Ted Shelton
Tracy Smith
Stephen Southerland
Dustin Stephens
Kurt Stolle
Aidan Stretch
Tricia Stuth
Susan Stump
Steve Tatge
Joyce Too
Sivichai Udomvoranun
Mark Vanderzanden
John Verdon
Eric Walter
Jennifer Wedderman
Holden Withington
Peter Wolff

*In addition, there have
been many interns,
students, and part-time
employees who have
contributed to the firm
over the years.*

BIOGRAPHIES

PARTNER TIMELINE

—

1977
David E. Miller and Robert E. Hull found the
Miller | Hull Partnership.
1985
Norman H. Strong is named managing partner.
1994
Craig A. Curtis is named partner.
2008
Ron Rochon, Scott Wolf, and Sian Roberts are
named partners.

DAVID E. MILLER, FAIA

—

Architect and founding partner of the Miller|Hull
Partnership, David Miller was born in Des Moines,
Iowa, in 1944. He received a bachelor of architecture degree in 1968 from Washington State
University. Miller spent the following two years
in the U.S. Peace Corps in Brasilia, Brazil, working
on self-help housing. On a Plym Fellowship,
he attended the University of Illinois, where he
received a master's in architecture in 1972.
During these years he worked part-time at the
Chicago office of Skidmore, Owings and Merrill.

After completing his graduate studies, Miller
worked one year for the Vancouver, Canada,
firm of Arthur Erikson on the British Columbia
Provincial Courthouse. In 1975 he joined Rhone
and Iredale Architects, where he was named partner and soon opened the RIA Seattle office with
Robert Hull. In 1977 the partners became inde-
pendent from RIA and renamed the firm the
Miller|Hull Partnership.

Miller joined the University of Washington in
1990 as an associate professor of architecture,
teaching graduate design studio. He was named a
fellow by the American Institute of Architects in
1994. In 1998 he received tenure at the university
and was advanced to the rank of full professor.
Currently, he is chair of the Department of
Architecture at the University of Washington.

In 2006 he received two distinctive awards:
the Washington State University Alumni Achievement Award and the BetterBricks Designer Award,
which recognized him as a designer who
supports, uses, and designs sustainable, high-
performance, commercial buildings.

ROBERT E. HULL, FAIA

—

Architect and founding partner of the Miller|
Hull Partnership, Robert Hull was born in
Moses Lake, Washington, in 1945. He received a
bachelor of architecture degree in 1968 from
Washington State University, twice receiving
the Student Distinction Award. From 1968
to 1972, Hull served in the U.S. Peace Corps in
Afghanistan, where he designed and built the
headquarters for the National Tourism Agency
and helped establish a school of architecture
at Kabul University.

After returning to the United States, he worked
in the New York office of Marcel Breuer from 1972
to 1975. He relocated to Vancouver, Canada, in
1975 to join Rhone and Iredale Architects, where
he was named partner. Hull was named a Fellow
by the American Institute of Architects in 1992.

Along with Miller in 2006, Hull received the
Washington State University Alumni Achievement
Award, which recognizes and honors alumni
who have given outstanding service and provide
encouragement to alumni for perpetual service
to Washington State University.

NORMAN H. STRONG, FAIA
LEED ACCREDITED PROFESSIONAL

—

Architect and partner, Norman Strong was born
in Moscow, Idaho, in 1954. He received a cum
laude bachelor of architecture degree in 1978
from Washington State University. He joined
Miller|Hull in 1979 and was named partner in
1985, assuming the role of managing partner
within the firm.

Active in the American Institute of
Architects (AIA), Strong was a board member of
the Washington State AIA Council as well as the
Northwest and Pacific Region of the AIA (2002–3).
In addition, he has served as AIA Seattle chapter
president (2000–1) and AIA vice president
and member of the board of directors (2005–7).
Most recently he has been leading the SDiG
(Sustainability Discussion Group), a national
AIA "road show" focused on listening and
getting out the word on AIA's sustainability blue-
print for America. Other community activities
have included serving on the advisory council of

the Washington State University School of Architecture, as well as being a board member and chair of the South District and West Seattle YMCA.

Strong was named a Fellow by the American Institute of Architects in 2004. He received the BetterBricks Advocate Award in 2007, which recognizes those who advocate for and support the design and operation of high-performance buildings, including consultants as well as workers in the government, nonprofit, and educational sectors.

CRAIG A. CURTIS, FAIA
LEED ACCREDITED PROFESSIONAL
—

Architect and partner of the Miller|Hull Partnership, Craig Curtis was born in Tonasket, Washington, in 1960. From Washington State University he received a cum laude bachelor of architecture degree in 1983 as well as a bachelor of science in construction management in 1984. He attended the Danish International Studies Program in Copenhagen, Denmark, in 1982.

After working at the Austin Hansen Fehlman Group in San Diego from 1984 to 1986, Curtis joined Miller|Hull in 1987, becoming the firm's first associate in 1989 and a partner in 1994. He has been the design partner on numerous award-winning Miller|Hull projects, and he has lectured on the firm throughout the country.

Curtis received the Jennie Sue Brown Award in 2004, the highest honor that can be bestowed by the AIA Washington Council. This "lifetime achievement" is given to an AIA Washington Council member who has, in a volunteer capacity, made a significant statewide contribution, served the profession, and enhanced the practice of architecture in a sustained manner. In 2008 he was named a Fellow by the American Institute of Architects.

SIAN ROBERTS, AIA
LEED ACCREDITED PROFESSIONAL
—

Architect and partner of the Miller|Hull Partnership, Sian Roberts was born in New York City in 1964. She earned her bachelor of science degree in physics at Haverford College in 1986 and her master's degree in architecture from the

University of Washington in 1991, where she received the Pio Prize for study at the University of Washington's Rome Center.

With more than twenty years of experience in architectural design, she has been with Miller|Hull since 1993 and is currently working on Miller|Hull's first BIM project, a design-build project of five community libraries for the King County Library System. She has taught design studio at the University of Washington and serves as a jury member on student reviews and design programs throughout the country. Roberts is a board member of the Seattle Architectural Foundation, where she is active in developing and maintaining youth programs, including downtown Seattle family tours, model building workshops, and school programs.

As leader of Miller|Hull's in-house green design team (known as Mixed Greens), Roberts supports and encourages continual exploration and integration of new sustainable products and ideas.

RON ROCHON, AIA
LEED ACCREDITED PROFESSIONAL
—

Quality control and construction administration services partner of the Miller|Hull Partnership, Ron Rochon was born in Everett, Washington, in 1957. From the University of Washington he received a bachelor of arts in architecture degree, cum laude, Phi Beta Kappa, in 1991, and a master of architecture degree in 1994. He was presented the Alpha Rho Chi Medal at the University of Washington in 1994 for his "demonstrated leadership, service, and the promise of professional merit." He participated in the University of Washington Italian Studies Program in Rome in 1992. After completing his master's degree, Rochon returned to Rome to be a graduate teaching assistant in 1994.

After working for Cardwell/Thomas and Associates, architects in Seattle from 1994 to 2000, Rochon joined Miller|Hull in 2000. He became principal in 2003 and partner in 2008. Although he has a role in nearly every project within the office, Rochon has a strong passion for environmental sustainability, energy efficiency, and renewable energy technologies, as well as projects that respond to the regional setting and climate. He is currently a member of the Seattle Public Utilities Water Systems Advisory Committee and the University of Washington Professionals Advisory Council.

SCOTT WOLF, AIA
LEED ACCREDITED PROFESSIONAL
—

Architect and partner of the Miller|Hull Partnership, Scott Wolf was born in Washington, D.C., in 1962. He is a 1984 graduate of North Carolina State University, where he received his bachelor of environmental design in architecture. He earned his master's degree in architecture from the University of Oregon in 1989.

Since joining the firm in 1993, Wolf has been an important contributor to Miller|Hull's rise to national leadership in sustainable design and the design for environmental education. He is currently responsible for the West Eugene Wetlands Environmental Education Center, targeting LEED Platinum and an Administration/Education Center and Laboratory for the LOTT Alliance, a wastewater treatment agency that is targeting LEED Platinum and Net Zero water and energy use in its new facility.

Wolf has taught at the University of Washington and regularly participates in student reviews at both the University of Washington and the University of Oregon. He has also served on a number of architecture and landscape architecture design awards juries. He coordinates Miller|Hull's commitment to the 1% solution (www.theonepercent.org) and spearheads the office Legacy Projects with the Columbia Land Trust, an organization that protects and conserves vital natural habitats along the Columbia River.

PHOTO CREDITS

SOUTH LAKE UNION DISCOVERY CENTER
Lara Swimmer: 19, 20, 21, 25, 27, 29 (top)
Miller|Hull: 29 (bottom)
Yoram Bernet: 22, 23, 28, 31

TECHNOLOGY ACCESS FOUNDATION
HEADQUARTERS AND COMMUNITY
LEARNING CENTER
Cesar Rubio: 42
Technology Access Foundation: 37
Yoram Bernet: 38 (model), 40 (model)

WILSONVILLE WATER TREATMENT
PLANT
Eckert & Eckert: 49,50, 51, 54–57, 58 (right), 60
    (bottom right), 62 (top), 64, 65
Nic Lehoux: 52, 53, 58 (left), 59, 60 (top and
    bottom), 61, 62 (bottom right), 63

TILLAMOOK FOREST CENTER
Loren Nelson: 76 (bottom). 77 (top: middle,
    right)
Miller|Hull: 71
Nic Lehoux: 67, 72–76 (top), 78, 79
Oregon Deparatment of Forestry: 68, 72

PIERCE COUNTY ENVIRONMENTAL
SERVICES BUILDING
Aiden Bradley: 84 (7; bottom right)
AldrichPears Associate: 93 (left)
Eckert & Eckert: 83 (bottom right), 89 (bottom
    right), 93 (right), 95 (right)
Nic Lehoux: 80, 83, 89, 90–93, 94, 95 (left),
    96, 97

KITSAP COUNTY ADMINISTRATION
BUILDING
Miller|Hull: 111
Nic Lehoux: 99, 101, 103–108, 110, 112, 113
Yoram Bernet: 101 (model), 109 (model)

FISHER PAVILION AT THE SEATTLE CENTER
C. Charles Bowden: 126 (6, 7, 9, 10)
Miller|Hull: 118 (top set), 126 (1, 2, 4, 5, 8)
Steve Keating: 115, 116, 120 (bottom left), 123,
    126 (3), 127
Yoram Bernet: 120 (top), 121, 124, 125, 128, 129

OLYMPIC COLLEGE–POULSBO
Chris Eden: 130
Nic Lehoux: 131, 133, 136, 139 (right, bottom,
    left), 148, 142, 143
Yoram Bernet: 135, 137, 139 (top left), 141

UNIVERSITY OF WASHINGTON CONIBEAR
SHELLHOUSE AND ATHLETIC CENTER
James Housel: 146
Miller|Hull: 148 (12), 156 (bottom middle)
Nic Lehoux: 145, 148 (5), 152, 154 (top), 155
    (right), 156 (top middle, right), 157–59
Yoram Bernet: 147, 148 (1), 150–52 (model), 154
    (bottom), 155 (left), 156 (top left)
University of Washington Libraries, Special
    Collections: 148 (2, 6, 7, 8–11)

ADDITION TO THE ART AND
ARCHITECTURE BUILDING, UNIVERSITY
OF MICHIGAN
Yoram Bernet: 169 (model), 170 (model)

1310 E. UNION LOFTS
Benjamin Benschneider: 180
Craig Richmond: 176
James F. Housel: 173, 177–79, 181

156 W. SUPERIOR STREET
Miller|Hull: 187 (bottom right), 193 (top right)
Nic Lehoux: 183, 187 (top), 188, 190–95
Yoram Bernet: 187 (model)